ALSO BY PATRICIA THORPE

Everlastings

THE
AMERICAN
WEEKEND
GARDEN

RANDOM HOUSE   NEW YORK

THE
AMERICAN
WEEKEND
GARDEN

PATRICIA
THORPE

Photographs by
Robert Gray and Richard S. Duncan
Illustrations by James Cardillo

Grateful acknowledgment is extended to Robert Gray and Richard S. Duncan, whose
photographs appear as follows:

Robert Gray: 143, 146, 147, 148, 151, 152, 153, 154, 155 above, 156 above, 158, 159, 160
above right, 162, 163 above, 166, 168 above right, 168 below, 169, 170, 171 above, 172, 173,
175 above, 178, 180 above, 181, 182, 184 above, 185, 186, 187 below.

Richard S. Duncan: 145 above, 149, 150, 155 below, 156 below, 157, 160 above left, 161, 163
below, 164, 165, 167, 171 below, 174, 175 below, 176, 177, 179 below, 180 below, 183, 187
above, 188, 189, 190.

Library of Congress Cataloging-in-Publication Data

Thorpe, Patricia.
The American weekend garden.

Bibliography: p.
1. Gardening–United States.   I. Title.
SB453.T485   1988   635′.0973   87-42671
ISBN 0-394-56025-6

Manufactured in the United States of America
24689753
First Edition

SPOT ILLUSTRATIONS AND BOOK DESIGN BY LILLY LANGOTSKY

For my father, John Thorpe,
the first weekend gardener in my life,
and still the best

C O N T E N T S

INTRODUCTION

Most American gardeners are weekend gardeners. Long working days, short vacations, long commutes and a shortage of reliable, knowledgeable gardening help have all contributed to this pattern and are factors not likely to change. In fact, with growing numbers of two-income families, weekend gardening is more than ever the way Americans garden. What is changing is the kind of garden Americans want to create.

Since World War II, gardening throughout the United States has been dominated by the idea of low maintenance. This reduced most suburban lots to expanses of lawn relieved only by foundation evergreens and a few spring-flowering trees. The range of perennial plants extended from hemerocallis to hosta; a few of the more daring homeowners put impatiens along the front walk.

Americans are fed up with the low-maintenance look. Urbanites buying country getaway cottages don't want them to look like the suburbs. And suburbanites are wondering if an acre of lawn and four capitata yews are reason enough for a three-hour commute.

The 1960's and 1970's, marked by an upsurge of enthusiasm for returning to the land, saw the beginning of the current second-home wave and renewed interest in backyard vegetable plots. This was an important step, because more people became aware that gardening was not necessarily routine drudgery like mowing the lawn—it could be creative, rewarding and fun. There are, however, definite creative limits to the vegetable garden. You have to start all over again every year. And the range of fascinating new vegetables you can grow, in spite of the claims of the seed catalogs, is pretty quickly exhausted. There's also no denying that even the most beautiful vegetable plot does little to transform the landscape setting of your home.

I think Americans want to grow flowers, to create picturesque cottage gardens bursting with color and variety throughout the seasons. They just don't really know where to start. And there is an oddly well-kept secret about this: Flowers are easy. Much easier than vegetables, particularly for gardeners who can work only a few hours a week. For one thing, there is a vast number of flowering plants that come back every year. I'm not sure why so many people find this surprising, but they do. Every year people visit my weekend garden, view the literally hundreds of varieties of flowers and timidly ask, "Do you put this in every year?" This confusion is excusable, since most Americans have been away from perennial flowering plants for so long, but still, I would have to be not only superhumanly industrious to plant a garden like mine every year, but also out of my mind.

A garden of perennial herbaceous plants and bulbs, hardy self-sowing annuals and biennials provides continual interest and excitement for much less work than vegetable gardens or plots of tender bedding plants like marigolds and petunias. This kind of garden also permanently transforms the setting of your home. These plants are the elements with which to create the American cottage garden.

The emphasis on American gardening is important. Although the great majority of would-be gardeners in this country are Anglophiles, American gardening has suffered in comparing itself to the English. We must look throughout our own countryside to find indigenous models; study our own spectacular landscape and develop ways of enhancing it; turn to the wealth of native plants we can use that Europeans simply cannot grow.

Gardening with hardy flowering plants is scarcely a new idea in this country, although it has been out of fashion for a few decades. There are gardens in most regions of America that still persist from the earlier part of this century, when there was a great deal more ornamental horticulture than there is today. There are still gardeners enjoying old-fashioned flowers which amaze everyone by returning every year. Seek out these indigenous gardens, however humble and unassuming they may first appear; look at them and learn about gardening in America. In a country of diverse and difficult climates, this is how you can learn what flowers will grow for you.

There are a few regions where old-fashioned local gardens may not exist. Often this is the case in areas more recently developed—the spectacular but inaccessible mountain and desert states of the West, for instance. Here gardeners must turn more to the astonishing scenery and unfamiliar but beautiful native flowers for inspiration for their gardens and for information on what plants to use.

This book is intended for weekend gardeners in every kind of situation, not simply for second-home owners. It's true that weekend refugees from our urban centers are becoming more interested in gardening—this is how I started my garden. But almost all suburban commuters, if they are gardeners at all, are weekend gardeners, and they have special problems to face in creating an interesting, beautiful and personal landscape.

Over and over this book stresses observing the surrounding landscape and learning from it. In the suburbs this landscape has all but vanished. The environment in many suburban areas has been reduced to small, uniform plots, each dotted with the same limited range of mass-market trees and shrubs. Although every inch is carpeted with grass or ground cover, and although foundation plantings glow with lurid color in the spring, many a suburban acre is as devoid of natural life as a gas station. A combination of town ordinances and peer pressure combine to make sure no one puts a meadow in place of the front lawn or starts a compost pile by the garage.

Some of the older suburbs, built before World War II, have interesting and beautiful plantings, but the greater expanses of suburbia as most of us know it were created when low maintenance was the overriding outdoor philosophy. It's not hard to grow things in the suburbs—just look at the luxuriant trees and grass. It's easier in some ways to garden there, since the overall manicured area produces fewer serious recurrent weed and insect problems than in the country. The hard part is getting away from the pervasive suburban outlook. The plots can be small and depressingly uniform. Any natural form the land may have had has been bulldozed. You don't have existing landscape features to help you out with your design as you might in the country. The problem is not that these yards are ugly. But they are without character—they reflect nothing of the part of the country they are in and nothing of the gardener who lives there.

The suburbs need the exuberance and variety that flowers can provide. They can benefit from the individuality that regional species offer. If you are a suburban gardener, the first step is to "loosen up" and explore new possibilities of design beyond the familiar pattern of lawn-tree-foundation planting. You could radically change these patterns if you make the effort—there are many more weekend gardeners living in the suburbs than anywhere else. It will take much imagination—one of the depressing aspects of the suburban look is its seeming inevitability; it looks persuasively as if nothing else could be done. Changing it will take nerve—peer pressure is not to be taken lightly. But for many, this is the closest you may come to "living in the country"; a creative approach to the outdoors can do much to bring a feeling of the country back to an undistinguished landscape. As Dr. Seuss says, I think you ought to try.

This is not a low-maintenance manual. This is a book for people who *want* to garden, who read books by Gertrude Jekyll and Margery Fish and fantasize about growing astrantia and campanula, but who really don't have much time to spend. Weekend gardeners have to find or make shortcuts, occasionally at the expense of the hallowed laws of "good garden practice." I should confess up front that my own attitude toward many aspects of basic upkeep is relaxed, to say the least. I feel that you can have an exuberant mass of flowers without being obsessive about edging, staking or keeping the bugs away. I probably don't mind enough when my plants fall over or when foxgloves spring up in the driveway. I don't mean to promote sloppy horticulture, but I do feel that an informal country garden should be able to suffer some indignities of upkeep and still be beautiful. Some of you might be horrified at the confusion in my own garden. Nonetheless, it continued to produce great quantities of flowers even when I spent a whole summer ignoring it (while I wrote this book). Feel free to be a lot more scrupulous than I recommend. A garden has to suit your own personality.

Will America ever really become a nation of gardeners? I want to believe it's possible, of course, but I realize that this is one way in which British horticulture may always have the advantage over us. In England, gardening is much more a fact of everyday life ("Like taking out the garbage," said one English horticulturalist). A house without flowers is like a house without rugs on the floor or pictures on the wall—you *can* live that way, but why would you want to? When you see parts of the United States where most people *do* have gardens (Charleston, South Carolina, or San Francisco and other parts of California), you can feel the strength of this attitude toward the out-of-doors—a garden is part of your home and part of your life. I will always be thankful for the pleasure of growing up with a similar point of view, since my father was one of the few suburban commuters of our area to have a real garden, all managed on the weekend. We grew up knowing that pansies had to be picked to keep them blooming, that asters should be planted in new soil every year, that roses had to be mounded in the fall, that peonies come back forever and tulips don't.

You can learn all these things from books, of course. What I couldn't have learned was much more essential: that gardening is an indispensable joy and that life without flowers is like life without friends or books or music—unthinkable. Few pleasures equal that of creating a living, flowering, permanent landscape. It may be many generations before this kind of thinking is again part of the American way of life, but you can discover this pleasure for yourself and you can make a gift of it to your children. I hope I succeed in sharing with you my own delight and excitement in making a garden.

A few more confessions: Not all the gardens pictured are weekend gardens. Please don't feel that this is some kind of fraud. They *are* all personal gardens managed by the one or two individuals who created them, not by professionals. All the plants shown and the ways that they are used are suitable for country gardens of little effort in many different parts of this continent. One problem with many new weekend gardens is that they are too ambitious. Too often beginning gardeners decide that the way to grow flowers is in an English border. The words "perennial" and "border" seem to have gotten welded together and many gardeners think that this is the only way they can grow flowers. Often, gardeners with more expertise are more nonchalant about how they use plants. Even if they have more time to spend on their gardens, they've discovered shortcuts to make their efforts go further. This is what we want to learn from the gardens shown in this book. These gardeners have discovered that the way to enjoy flowers is not just in one big bed but in all parts of a flowering landscape. We can take a little shortcut and imitate some of their creative ideas.

Of course, some of the "gardens" shown are not really gardens at all, but just examples of sturdy perennials that have naturalized and returned to decorate farmyards and abandoned lots. These are shown as examples of the kind of persistent flowers you should look for in your own area when you are deciding what you can grow.

These photographs are also a testament to hardy plants in a terrible climate. The summer these pictures were taken was one of the worst for gardens in the East. Severe drought ravaged the South. In the North, late and early frosts resulted in one of the shortest growing seasons in decades—in my own area, only ninety days without frost.

On the second of June, with the garden in full bloom, the temperature was 28°. I watched in tears as hundreds of flowers slowly melted into the consistency of wet tissue paper. If I had been doing a book on half-hardy bedding annuals I would have thrown in the trowel at that point. But many of the pictures were taken less than three weeks later and prove that my garden and many others were far from lost. This kind of gardening disaster is common in many parts of our country. I hope it doesn't happen often to you, but even if it does, you can still make a garden that will survive.

I should say a few words about botanical nomenclature. I am a wholehearted believer in Latin binomials. If you are going to garden at all seriously, it is important that you learn and use the correct name of a plant; otherwise you will never know what you are growing or buying. On the other hand, most readers, including myself, stop cold when they see a line of Latin italics stretching across the page like a string of barbed wire. The pattern of Latin name followed by parenthetical common name is extremely repetitious. For the most part, I use the generic name of a plant, occasionally replacing it with the common name for variety or interest. Most species are listed with both Latin and common names in Appendix A. I fear that in trying to make this book friendly and approachable, I may have let down Linnaeus and L. H. Bailey, but next time, perhaps, I'll do it right.

THE
AMERICAN
WEEKEND
GARDEN

1

· · ·

GETTING
YOUR BEARINGS

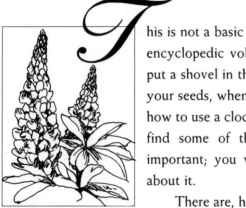

This is not a basic gardening book. There are numerous encyclopedic volumes that describe in detail how to put a shovel in the ground, how to scarify and stratify your seeds, when to take chrysanthemum cuttings and how to use a cloche. As a beginning gardener you may find some of this information interesting or even important; you will have to look elsewhere to read about it.

There are, however, some aspects of garden-making that are even more basic than using that shovel, and things you should consider long before you try to start those seeds. In general, this book is long on thinking, short on working—this is an important division of labor in a weekend garden.

If you have just bought your suburban or country home, you probably have months or years of work ahead of you, making the house comfortable or even livable. Don't be in a hurry to take on the out-of-doors, especially if you have no experience in gardening. A garden is an extremely long-range project;

another year or two of just getting your bearings is worth the wait. Try to get the plumbing under control, fix the roof, get the water out of the basement; while you're dealing with the usual catastrophes of homeowning, take long walks; get to know local wild flowers; see what (if anything) your neighbors are growing. While the polyurethane is drying on the floors, sit out in the grass and get some sense of what your property is like.

LEARNING TO LOOK — SEEING THE LANDSCAPE

Most of your time as an about-to-be weekend gardener should be spent just looking. It is overwhelmingly likely that you have no experience in seeing nature, no real notion about how to approach plants and the environments in which they live. You are far from alone in this inexperience—it's unfortunately true throughout our country. Happily, it is easily changed, once you start to pay attention to the world around you. Looking at plants and gardens is like looking at art or architecture or anything else—if it is done consciously, and if it is done all the time, even a person with no formal education in the subject can learn an enormous amount and, more important, develop a personal taste and enjoyment of it that is vastly more valuable than anything that can be learned from a book. You can read about how to double-dig a bed and how many pounds of lime to use on your lawn; no book can tell you how to utilize those awkward hummocks that make up your backyard to create a fascinating planted reflection of the rolling hills surrounding you. Look at pictures in gardening books—they can provide information on the wide range of gardening styles available, but they are more important in showing you how to look at and think about gardens. Visit gardens, any and all gardens, and see how they succeed or fail. Don't be afraid to realize that many gardens are terrible—they will continue to be so until people really learn to see what makes a garden wonderful. This is total heresy for a garden writer, of course, and I do appreciate that it is better for people to make terrible gardens than no gardens at all. But until we approach gardening seriously and critically it can never be seen as it should: as an art, one of the great arts, much less ephemeral than ballet or haute cuisine and more available to everyone. The Japanese see it that way; the British obviously do; and the result is evident in the gardens those cultures have produced.

Don't get panicked that you are going to be expected to make a masterpiece in your weekend garden. We're starting slowly, and starting small, with fairly limited expectations. The first step is to look.

Learn about your own response to the countryside. Anyone can respond to the spectacular, of course; try to look more closely at the details of a landscape. Why do certain scenes appeal to you? Is your ideal landscape a scene of Constable or the overdramatic but highly realistic Catskill scenery of the Hudson River school?; Georgia O'Keeffe or Elliot Porter? Your feelings about this influenced which property you bought, consciously or not; these feelings can be used to give direction to the way your garden develops.

Discover the everyday flowers around you, in and out of gardens. In a general way these can indicate your personal bias toward or against broad types of plants. I for one love the graceful cobwebby effect of vines around houses and over trees; many of you may just find them messy. Great numbers of gardeners can't have enough azaleas and rhododendron—that group of shrubs leaves me completely cold.

Natural combinations of roadside weeds can inspire plantings in your garden—if something catches your eye, stop (traffic permitting) and try to figure out what it is. If you like the cheerful yellow of dandelions in early spring but are embarrassed to let them take over your lawn, carpet a damp, semishaded corner with the brilliant gold of marsh marigolds. Look at the drifts of chicory and Queen Anne's lace along the highway, like a brilliant blue sky with clouds; don't let them into your garden, but re-create the effect with nigella (love-in-a-mist) and baby's breath, or campanula and achillea.

You don't need acres to make a weekend garden: Here flowering shrubs and perennials transform a typical subdivision lot into a backyard that feels like the country. One daunting aspect of lots like these is their lack of distinguishing features. Create your own with architectural elements like this arbor seat, which breaks up boring expanses of space and makes a perfect planting site.

Get a sense of the overall effect of your house in the landscape. Is it a stark and elegant glass box perched on a rock by the sea or a quiet cottage nestled in a woodland? It might be a stately old home in a small town or a ruined farmhouse with acres of open fields. You could be starting from scratch on a half-acre subdivision. Each situation will require different plans and different plants.

A few more specific questions: Where is the sun at different times of the day and how many hours of full sunlight can you expect in different parts of what might be your garden? Do you have shade? Too much, too little? Is it the open dappled shade of high trees or the bleak north side of a building? There are flowers for all different levels of light, but get some idea now about how much sun goes where. Is there a lot of wind, and is it always from one direction? (The local airport can help you with that one.) Are there areas of ground that are always damp and spongy, even after weeks of dry weather? Are there changes of level from one area to another? Are there views out you might want to clear away or frame? What about views *in*—do you want your neighbors supervising your laundry or badminton games? Consider the age and activities of your family—is a sandbox a necessity or a soccer field?

There is one basic question only you can answer—how do you like to spend your time? If skiing is your favorite sport and you spend all summer sitting around waiting for the snow to fall again, you may have a lot of time and energy to put into a garden. If you're out all weekend on your boat you had better stick to the low-maintenance formula of trees and shrubs. You will be creating a garden slowly, little by little, and you can always decide when you've had enough, but have some idea before you start if this is going to fit into your weekend plans.

It is more the exception than the norm, but you may have bought a house that already has a garden of some sort. It's tempting to think of having this all ready-made, but it is more than likely not a garden you would want: Perhaps it's a vegetable plot smack in the middle of a possible volleyball site or fussy little beds of annuals cut out of the front lawn. Heaven help you, it might be one of the petunia-and-marigold mounds so beloved in some areas. It very likely includes some form of foundation planting you are better off without. If you are very lucky it could be big patches of daffodils that have been there forever, a few peonies as old as the house, maybe a line of iris along the walk. With these we can do something, although probably not what was done by the previous owner. Existing shrubs and perennial plants are very useful in several ways—they give specific information on what will live in your climate and soil, and they give you a head start on possible plant material. Just don't feel you have to live with someone else's garden. Plants can always be moved—sometimes with difficulty, it's true, but it's better to take the chance than feel stuck with something in the wrong place. Don't be timid about disposing of things you can't stand—give those rhododendron away if you hate them.

YOUR CLIMATE AND YOUR GARDEN

Weekend gardening is in most respects like any kind of gardening except in the crucial factors of time and work expenditures. Gardeners have always been able to vary, within limits, the growing conditions around them, but the extent to which this is done is directly controlled by the amount of work spent doing it. To put it plainly: It is far easier to grow plants that are successful in your climate. Two essentials in successful weekend gardening are, therefore, understanding your climate and finding plants that thrive within its limitations.

Climate defines culture: This is one of Toynbee's basic premises, and it makes me suspect he was a gardener. Before you became a gardener, climate probably meant little more to you than the morning weather forecast and the question of an umbrella or not. One of the ways gardening enhances your understanding of the natural world is the enormous change it makes in your awareness of weather and what it means. It's very likely that you have been living in ignorance of the frost dates of your area and their significance. Do you know the length of your growing season? Is your average annual rainfall twenty inches or sixty? What's the degree difference in daytime and nighttime temperatures? Do you have a period of winter dormancy and if so, how long?

You don't have to know all this before you start your garden, and much of it will slowly become part of the subconscious knowledge you possess as you live with gardening and the out-of-doors. But a general understanding of these crucial factors can save you a lot of effort and disappointment in the early stages of your experimentation. It could be the difference between creating a beautiful country landscape and giving up in despair in two years.

All of us beginning gardeners are enthralled and intimidated by the great institution of English gardening, so it might be useful to examine the climatic factors that contribute to its splendor and contrast them with those that affect American gardening. The British climate is uniquely suited to horticulture. Overall the temperatures are as mild as those of our most southern states, but with no prolonged hot spells or periods of drought. The winters are cool enough and long enough to provide dormancy for most plants, but prolonged periods of severe cold are unknown, even in the mountain areas. The growing and flowering season is long—March to November in many areas—and precipitation is generously provided throughout. If this sounds a little like Camelot to you, keep in mind that there's not much good beach weather, and ski resorts don't do very well; the winters are incredibly dark, wet and depressing, and the summers can provide weeks without one gloriously sunny day; the plants, however, couldn't be happier. It would be naive to think that the rich tradition of English gardening, stretching back as it does throughout their history and cutting across all levels of society, developed independently of this marvelous climate for growing things. Now, not all British gardens are beautiful—the British are just as capable of bad taste as anyone else and in certain periods of garden history have produced monstrosities—but almost everyone gardens, and almost everything grows. This can't help but produce a uniformly high level of horticulture.

American gardeners, in case you hadn't noticed, don't have it so easy. In fact, when you review some of the statistics, it seems incredible that anyone can grow anything, much less create the splendid agricultural nation America was until industry and changing social patterns diminished its importance in that field. The American climate is a broad patchwork of every kind of extreme. The areas that are mild are also very hot; the areas of cold have a cold unknown in Western Europe. The growing seasons are short; where they are long they are frequently interrupted by periods of total drought. Even places with good yearly rainfall—thirty to forty inches—often have this distributed across three or four months, leaving the rest of the year dry. The extremes vary enormously from one part of the country to another, but there is also enormous range within one state or even one county.

A few statistics may make these extremes more concrete. Lovely North Carolina has, from many points of view, an ideal climate. The growing season is long—around or more than 200 days, April through October. (The term "growing season" is used here to refer to the period of the year without frost. Obviously many plants grow—and flower—before and after frost, but this is a general indication of the season for the greatest number of plants.) Rainfall is excellent, forty-five to fifty inches a year or more, and occurs evenly throughout the year. The average January temperatures are mid-30's to mid-40's; July temperatures average in the high 70's. Sounds just about perfect for man or plant alike and yet every part of the state has periods—usually short—between 0° and 10°, and many places experience nights between 0° and –20°; every county has days above 100° and 103°–106° days are not unknown.

Arizona has a growing season that can be more than 300 days or less than 150, depending on your part of the state. In any part of Arizona you would be lucky to get twenty inches of rain; something less than ten is more routine. The temperate January averages are 40°–50° or above; less appealing July has averages of mid-to-high 80's into mid-90's, and temperatures above 100° are unspeakable but not unusual.

My own state of New York is not often counted among the harshest climates in the Union; still, in my county the growing season is usually less than 140 days—among the shortest in the United States—and the average January temperature is 20°. Temperatures of –20° to –30° are not rare enough. Average yearly snowfall is sixty to eighty inches. Then, again, I could try to garden in Wyoming in a growing season of less than sixty days with a possible temperature spread from –38° to 105° and eleven inches of rain.

I hope you are neither bored by these statistics nor discouraged (actually, if I lived in Wyoming, I'd be a little discouraged). I want to use these numbers to demonstrate two things. First, even with a cruel and unusual climate you can grow many plants successfully—widespread and diverse agriculture takes place in every part of the United States, and no state is without its own beautiful native vegetation. Second, it is extremely hard to make sweeping generalizations about gardening in America. I have gardened in several states and lived and visited many others, but a book really always has one overall viewpoint. Special sections on specific areas of the United States are provided to offset this to some extent, but one of the aims of this book has been not to try to tell you about your own climate but to enable you to analyze your environment and learn to figure out for yourself what will grow in it.

HOW PLANTS COPE—OR DON'T

How does climate affect plant selection? Climate extremes can make it difficult or impossible for certain plants to survive. Cold weather can freeze plant tissues, retard bud or fruit formation, split bark and force roots out of the ground. Extremes of heat will often slow the rate of growth of a plant and dwarf it. Some plants will produce only leaves; some plants, if they do produce flowers or fruit, do so prematurely, so flowers are stunted and fruit is tasteless and poor in color and size. Winter dormancy is necessary for some plants—cold and shortened days combine to trigger this necessary resting period; without it, plants bloom erratically, if at all, and usually die after a few years. This happens frequently when gardeners try to take northern favorites south for retirement. Summer dormancy is found among the native plants of the West and Southwest—these plants, perfectly suited to their environment, need a summer rest of absolute dryness.

Plants have various methods of dealing with climate extremes. One strategy is to complete the entire cycle of reproduction, seed-plant-flower-seed, in one growing season. These plants we call annuals. Cosmos, cleome and calendula are attractive examples, well suited to a country garden.

Some plants, biennials, take two years to complete a cycle. Typically, seeds germinate midseason and a young plant is established by the onset of cold weather. Often these plants will bloom early the following spring, seed ripens by midsummer and the cycle starts again. The original plant dies. Digitalis (foxglove) is a familiar example of a biennial. In this case the pattern of growth enables the plant to bloom in cool, early summer weather when temperatures suit it best. In a cool climate like that of England or the mountains of South America, where foxgloves have naturalized freely, or in the Pacific Northwest, this plant will continue to bloom over a long period. Although it will survive in a warmer climate, flowering will stop when the temperatures rise. Some western American plants like oenothera utilize the biennial habit to endure midsummer heat and drought.

Perennial plants may bloom the second year from seed but most take several years to reach their full stature. In spite of being called perennials, most have a limited life span, although some, like peonies, seem to live forever and make more enormous flowering masses every year. In cold climates the entire plant of a perennial above ground may die back completely, only to reappear, miraculously, in the spring. In hot climates, this occurs during heat and drought. This yearly spectacle is as moving as it is mysterious, and it is part of the fascination of perennial plants.

Woody plants—trees and shrubs, deciduous or evergreen—have even more sophisticated dormancy procedures, since the woody framework of the plant persists above ground through the winter. This makes them more susceptible to injury from cold; their climate range is somewhat more inflexible for this reason. The broadleaf evergreens in particular have very definite limits to where they can grow.

"Hardiness" is a term much used in horticulture, and one that seems to have a bewildering variety of definitions. Throughout this book it is used to refer to a plant's ability to withstand cold. We will discover many other ways in which plants can fail to survive certain conditions, but cold is the most widespread climate problem in this country and the most unchangeable. The U.S. Department of Agriculture has divided the United States into ten climate zones on the basis of temperature lows—the map on page 269 illustrates this division. These zone numbers are widely used and are becoming more so as perennial plants return in popularity; they are a useful shorthand for a plant's hardiness. Remember, however, that they take into account only the factor of cold. Remember also that the number refers to the coldest zone in which a plant will live, not the coldest zone in which it will bloom. A plant like tricyrtis may survive Zone 4 winters, but because it blooms in October the flowers freeze in many areas. The familiar *Cornus florida*, the flowering dogwood, and forsythia can both withstand cold, but since the buds are carried on the plants through the winter and since flower parts often freeze before the woody parts of the plants, neither tree nor shrub blooms in the colder parts of our country. At the other end of the range, cold-hardy eastern shrubs like deutzia or lilac *can* grow in California, but because of their need for winter dormancy, their bloom is sporadic and adds little in this landscape where so much flourishes. There is often no way of knowing from its hardiness rating how a plant will respond to extremes of heat. You can see that although these zone numbers are enormously helpful and should be even more widely used than they are, they are far from the whole story.

Man the gardener, in his infinite urge to grow an ever broader range of plants, has developed techniques for restructuring a plant's habit of growth to cheat on climate limitations. These techniques, while often not complicated or difficult, require more time and effort than most of us weekenders want to spend; I'm going to discuss them briefly, however, because they involve terms that you will commonly see in gardening books or seed catalogs, and they produce some of our most familiar plants.

We now know what an annual is. A tropical or semitropical annual cannot tolerate frost and requires a longer period of growth than is provided in most of North America. If the plant is exposed to cold—often it doesn't even have to be freezing—either in spring or fall, it dies. These plants are called tender or half-hardy annuals. To be successful in a colder climate, these plants must start their cycle of growth in midwinter or very early spring, and obviously they must start it indoors. These tender annuals include many of our most familiar "garden-center specials" and are unfortunately the most commonly grown flowers in America. Growers start them in midwinter in greenhouses; you buy them in May or June, plant them out after the last frost (you hope) and have them until the first fall freeze. Impatiens, African marigolds and zinnias are examples of half-hardy annuals.

Half-hardy biennials or perennials are more of a problem. What is the point in nurturing a plant through its first unproductive year if it's not going to live to bloom the second? Some of these plants, if started very early, will bloom the first year—these are used as annuals and many gardeners don't know the difference. Pelargoniums (what we usually call geraniums) are a good example. In a mild climate it is easy to see that these are perennial—they make woody, shrublike masses in California. Some of these plants can be grown indoors through the winter; some, like dahlias or gladiolus, can be stored above ground in a dormant state. All this is complicated and a fair amount of work—leave tender perennials to frost-free gardeners in the South.

There is no question that hardiness is a crucial factor in American gardening but it's not nearly as limiting as it sounds, once you understand it. Yet many gardeners in America have thrown up their hands at the whole problem and now confine their gardening ambitions to growing the same six or eight tender annuals, the garden-center specials. I don't hate these plants (though you'll hear me disparage them endlessly). I just resent the idea that they are all Americans can grow. It would be dreadful if every house we went into had one of six possible wallpapers, if we all wore one of eight possible uniforms every day. But this is how Americans in recent years have dressed the surroundings of their homes, and this is what we are going to change in our weekend gardens.

It is only with flowers that persist from year to year that one can create a landscape and a garden. Perennial plants make it possible to grow an immeasurably greater number and variety of flowers, even if you just garden on the weekends. A perennial garden grows and changes one week to the next throughout its long season. Instead of facing the same dutiful line of petunias every Friday night, you could experience the excitement of a whole new assortment of plants coming into blossom each week. Perennials lengthen the time you can enjoy your garden—instead of waiting for Memorial Day to set out your geraniums, you could have been enjoying tiny bulbs and rock-garden plants that start as soon as the snow melts.

A flowering garden is not just made up of perennials—trees, shrubs, vines, annuals and bulbs should all have a place in the weekend garden. I am placing particular emphasis on perennials because they have been neglected in the past few decades of gardening in America, and they are now beginning to make a tentative comeback. Flowering trees and shrubs, luckily, are so easy to care for that they remained in the gardening repertoire even through the doldrums of low-maintenance suburban gardening. Trees and shrubs are vital to any kind of landscape decor—they provide the overall structure for our outdoor life—but to make an American cottage garden (which is how we secretly dream about our weekend homes) we need flowers. Lots of different flowers, making masses of fragrance and color and carrying on all summer. You can do this with annuals but only to a much more limited extent—annuals just take much more work. If an American weekend gardener wants flowers, perennials are the answer. This is why understanding your climate is so important. And that's why the next step is preparing the soil.

If plants are going to live more or less permanently in your garden, somewhat more soil preparation is necessary than for short-lived annuals or vegetables. Perennial plants often have deep and massive root systems that need accommodation; nutritional elements must be available in the soil and must be replenished periodically. Perennials will need water, too, but in this respect they are much less demanding than annuals once they are established; their more elaborate root systems drain a larger surface area, reach deeper, and often are designed to store moisture. The crucial factor involving water is drainage. This could be defined roughly as the ability of moisture to move through the soil. In sandy soils water drains very rapidly—spongelike organic material (compost, manure, peat moss) must be added to hold some moisture and make it available to the plants. Soil that doesn't drain well is, unfortunately, much more common. Often a subsoil layer of compressed clay and rock causes the water to collect in puddles around the roots of the plant. If your so-called topsoil is mostly clay, it will congeal around the roots in sticky, airless lumps. Perhaps a high water table in your area keeps a constant underground bog just beneath your beds. Any of these conditions can be fatal to plants. Annual flowers and vegetables may slog through a summer in these conditions, but few plants will survive extended periods this way. Good drainage can often extend the hardiness range of a plant, sometimes by a whole climate zone, but poor drainage is a death warrant for almost anything that spends a winter in the ground. Yes, there are some hardy water dwellers—you can create a whole garden of these lovely specimens (page 208). But in the beginning, assume that almost everything needs to be well drained—few of your plants will resent it.

Thinking about drainage is a little like trying to figure out how all that water got into your basement, and how you are going to get it out. A great deal about drainage can be understood with plain common sense. Water on its way from one place to another is not usually a problem; once it stops moving it causes trouble. For this reason, one easy way around the drainage question is planting areas of ground higher than those surrounding. Planting on sloping ground can also be effective. Sometimes, however, even high ground can trap water if an impermeable layer of rock hardpan underlies the topsoil. This is not difficult to determine; if you dig down eighteen inches or so and suddenly hit soil like concrete, this is your problem. Often you can break through this layer and hit more permeable soil beneath. If you are on high ground, this is all the incentive the water needs to move on. If all you have beneath your hardpan is hardpan, however, you may have to dig out the whole planting area and lay channels of drainage tile to direct the water elsewhere. If you are planting only a single tree or shrub, you can dig down deep and make a gravel-filled well beneath the root ball. This will help to hold water away from most of the roots and the crown of the plant.

After a little investigation, you can usually tell what parts of your property are likely to be drainage problems. If you dig a hole when the topsoil is of normal dryness but you hit water as you go down, the location sounds like a bad bet. If you have fairly varied terrain, you can probably find some places that are better than others. If all your land is low-lying and swampy, consider digging down in the lowest spot and making a small pond. This will tend to drain off higher areas, and excess soil from the excavation can be used to create raised beds above the pool. Raised beds are useful in a variety of difficult drainage situations: This is one way to escape a high water table and avoid confrontation with underlying rock or hardpan. Raised beds or terraces supported by drywall retaining walls offer even greater opportunity for getting the water out.

Soil preparation works hand in hand with drainage techniques to keep water from settling in. I never knew water could stand in puddles on the side of a steep hill until I discovered upstate clay. When it's wet, heavy clay soil holds water around the roots and crowns of plants; when it's dry (this is a frequent condition in the West) water bounces off the surface and never reaches the plant. Clay soil, like sandy soil, needs quantities of organic matter; besides the compost and manure, clay soil can benefit from the addition of sand or light gravel. This creates spaces between soil particles so the soil can breathe; this also enables water to move more freely.

Whole chapters—whole books, even—have been written about soil: the complicated chemical and biological processes going on underground, the delicate balancing of the pH scale, etc. If this is the kind of thing you like, there's a lot you can learn and work on. (See the Bibliography for suggested books on the subject.) A soil analysis to determine your garden's pH is helpful and not difficult to do—either with a home kit or by taking a sample to your county extension agent—but don't be surprised if this factor makes little difference to your gardening in the long run. Many "dirt gardeners" don't know one end of the pH scale from the other. In a very general way you can tell if your area is more acid or alkaline (limy): Blueberries and strawberries, gentians, moss and conifers indicate a somewhat acid disposition. For years I assumed our soil must have lots of lime; the grass flourishes without ever being limed, and the lilacs, well-known lime lovers, are spectacular. Well, turns out the grass is gorgeous because the climate favors it, and everyone dumps wood ashes on the lilacs. Our soil is acid after all. Fifteen years of growing thousands of kinds of plants have gone on without my knowing this; some plants do well, some don't, but then, that's always the case. In places where the soil is *very* acid or alkaline, it is worth the effort to try to bring the pH closer to neutral, since that will support the greatest variety of plants. Lime neutralizes acid soil, aluminum sulfate "sweetens" alkalinity. In most soils, however, good general preparation—providing proper drainage and adding quantities of organic material—will slowly neutralize the ground. There is only a relatively small number of plants that are really fussy about pH one way or the other and most of them are difficult for any number of reasons—these are not plants for the weekend garden. It is easier to add lime to slightly acid soil to suit certain plants than it is to try to grow acid lovers on chalk—the lime keeps leaching through the soil.

In many ways soil is much easier to deal with than climate. It's tangible, and you can do something about it, and you *have* to do something about it to prepare for growing your plants: Sandy soil must be made less porous; clay soil must be made to breathe. All beds must be made to drain. Organic material must be provided. But in some ways your soil should be accepted the way your climate is. It's important to know about its specific conditions, and to understand them. And some of those conditions, e.g., drainage, will have to be changed to grow anything. But don't drive yourself crazy trying to grow Japanese iris or gentians in limy soil. Be happy instead with gypsophila, dianthus and lilacs.

You are probably becoming convinced that your climate will never allow much more than dandelions and burdocks and your soil is better suited for making bricks than growing plants. All gardeners go through this—it is a gardener's privilege and obligation to complain about his growing conditions. Believe me, you can have a wonderful weekend garden and you can find many more fascinating flowers to flourish in your garden than you will ever have time or space for. They may not be the plants you first thought you wanted to grow: I was upset that my forsythia was a disaster and every year my lilies get frostbite. The delphinium, on the other hand, effortlessly tops eight feet and my edelweiss looks like a photo on a Swiss calendar. An early September freeze eliminates chrysanthemums but provides fall foliage that rivals any flowers. Learn to lose gracefully and learn to love your growing conditions with all their limitations. They are helping you to create a garden that is your own.

2
. . .
SHAPING A
FLOWERING LANDSCAPE

he design of your garden and the selection of plant material are the two major factors in creating a garden you can manage and enjoy on the weekends. These two factors work reciprocally, and it's not easy to discuss one without the other. We will talk about planning your garden first, but keep in mind that working with natural elements, elements with lives of their own, is completely different from designing, for instance, the interior of your home. If you decide on the perfect sofa or rug for your living room, it may or may not be exactly what you thought you wanted, but at least it will stay where you put it and remain more or less the same color. Chances are it won't disappear overnight or change shape or start to multiply and take over the room. Plants can do any of those things— don't be surprised, shocked or hurt when they do. You may carefully map out your plans for the landscape, but remember that the material which makes up the design will constantly be modifying, reshaping or abandoning your program.

A successful plan for a weekend garden must retain enough flexibility to respond to the vagaries of plant life. It must also be compatible with the land in which it develops. Landscapes in a more or less natural state are amazingly specific; the elements which make them up are both extremely numerous and diverse. This makes it very hard to speak about garden design in anything but the vaguest terms. It's even worse than writing about architecture or interior design—at least there you could assume such central elements as floors, walls and ceilings. Bear with the generalizations, then, and when you feel confused, go outside, walk around and get back in touch with your land.

Design may be a somewhat intimidating word for what we want to do, which is to shape your property into a flowering landscape. Too often new gardeners have too limited an idea of how flowers can make a garden. Forget you ever saw a flower bed; pretend the words "perennial border" don't exist. We are going to find ways of using many kinds of flowering plants, and we're going to use them everywhere. Your garden should be everything that surrounds you—it shouldn't be confined to one narrow strip along the edge of the lawn.

Because your garden involves all your outdoor space, it is useful to think about various utilitarian demands on this space before you plan your plantings. Plants do have various requirements about their growing conditions, but these can almost always be adjusted; the requirements of a tennis court usually can't be. Often there is only one likely place to park your car or store the garbage. These may seem boring considerations when all you want to do is get out and plant flowers, but that's all the more reason to get these matters over with early. You can always put a trellis of wisteria around the trash area, once you decide where it has to be. Plantings often develop best from problem solving.

Even after siting the functional parts of your outdoor life, you may still be left with a lot of formless open space. The sheer size of it all is perplexing; half an acre is far larger than any living room any of us have ever had to arrange, and an acre or more can seem a vast and terrifying expanse. The first impulse is usually to divide, enclose and otherwise limit all this space, and this tendency is endorsed by several centuries of garden history. Few of us have not looked with longing at Italian or English gardens surrounded by walls of ancient brick or stone. These gardens are very approachable, much more like rooms than the out-of-doors; in such a garden the size and shape is defined and laid out—a gardener need only furnish it with flowers.

You've probably noticed that this kind of garden is extremely rare in the American countryside, but perhaps that's just as well. There are many other ways of enclosing your garden, once you decide that's what you want to do, but look carefully at your property before you decide. So much of the natural scenery of America is magnificent; if your country property shares some of this splendor, the last thing you want to do is fence yourself in. Spaces can be defined without being confined. One of the most noticeable characteristics of the photographs in this book is the way the gardens are open to the landscape around them. This doesn't mean that you have to perch a perennial border on some windswept pinnacle, or even that you have to be staring out at the same spectacular view all the time. But you can shape your space so that natural beauty around you enhances what you plant. The Japanese use the term "borrowed scenery" for this technique, and it can work well in the American country garden.

A QUESTION OF STYLE:
FORMAL VERSUS INFORMAL GARDENS

Although there are many different styles your garden can employ, one fundamental division is formal versus informal. It is a question of strong personal taste which you prefer, but I should warn you right here that an informal garden (and gardening) style is much more compatible with a weekend garden. Formal gardening demands enormous control over your plant material and that control is the direct result of a lot of effort. The landscape does not, in general, lay itself out in straight lines. Most plants, when left to themselves, don't assume neat geometrical shapes. They don't all grow to the same size and they don't stand up straight. They can be made to do these things but at the price of constant upkeep. You can, if your land permits, have regular spaces instead of oddly shaped ones; your paths can be straight and paved with brick; you can use cut stone instead of natural rocks. All these decisions can lend a formal air to your setting without requiring any more work than the alternatives. Just don't try to impose this formality on your plants. A few species of trees and shrubs have nicely symmetrical shapes and these can lend emphasis to your outline, but you will have a very limited plant list if this is the only kind of plant you want. As a weekend gardener, you have to learn to leave a great deal of gardening to your plants—see the way they grow and let your garden develop from that. Geometric shapes require shaping; sharply defined edges need edging; formal paving demands that no intrusive weeds spring up between the bricks. The overall effect in a formal garden depends on everything in its place—the wheelbarrow or express wagon can't be left out on the lawn, and the hose is used only discreetly after dark.

I personally have great admiration for the grand formal gardens of bygone eras but I don't think they offer workable models for Americans of today with little time and no help. If you are determined to shape at least part of your garden this way, keep it small. You may be amazed how much time will be required maintaining even a very limited area in this fashion. The rest of us will be content with informality ranging from the cheerfully nonchalant to the practically chaotic.

WHITHER GOEST THOU: PATHS AND BYWAYS

How do you go about shaping space? If most of the property around your home is open, with some outstanding features, start with a few paths. Ask yourself some existential-sounding questions: Where are you going and what do you do when you get there? Paths direct movement, but they also direct the eye and arouse interest about other parts of the garden; besides, they are excellent locations for plantings in themselves. But there are few things more irritating than a path that goes nowhere, or one that does everything to keep you from where you want to go. No one wants to meander to the woodpile or toolshed—walks like this can be attractive, but they must be direct. In contrast, stepping-stones through the rock garden should slow traffic for careful viewing.

Before you lay out your paths, see where your steps take you naturally. Let the grass grow up in your lawn or field, then trace your favorite routes with a lawn mower. See what spaces are made by these outlines, then think about how they can be emphasized by plantings. One long straight avenue might be made into an allée; an open rectangle might be outlined by shrub plantings. An awkward incline may be just the place for a few steps to mark the change in level.

If, instead of a great open field or an open suburban plot your property is more like virgin forest, you can still follow the same program but use a chain saw instead of lawn mower. Decide first how much of this woodland you want to live with. You can preserve most of it and simply create a lovely shade garden (look for suggestions on page 202). But if you want a more varied terrain with more varied plant material, some of the trees have to go. Proceed slowly—the existing trees and shrubs will give definition to your newly created spaces and fine old trees give a feeling of permanence to a garden that can't be equaled by new planting, however lovely. If you level too much at once, you may just end up planting more trees from scratch like the rest of us.

MAKING THE MOST OF WHAT YOU'VE GOT

Existing features of your property can give purpose to the movement through your garden. Any spectacular view will be a magnet, so build up to it in different ways; it's best if it can be seen from only some parts of the garden. Water of any kind is irresistible; besides drawing people to it, it makes possible plantings very different from the rest of your garden. Changes of level add interest, especially if they are emphasized with steps, terraces or retaining walls, all of which make excellent planting sites.

There are so many possible landscape features that I can't begin to offer enough examples—you really must determine for yourself what assets your property possesses. These features can be natural or man-made—large trees or shrub clusters; walls, arbors, fences; rock outcroppings; streams, mudholes or ponds; barns or sheds. Any or all can provide varied planting sites for flowers and become part of the garden scheme.

Of course, if you feel that you really don't have anything around which to build your garden, all is not lost. If you have never witnessed the inspiring and terrifying effects wrought by a bulldozer or backhoe, you may feel you have to accept your land as it is, but you don't. Hills can be pushed around; changes of level can appear on the flattest plot; ponds can be dug and streams diverted. These are clearly major structural changes and should not be taken on without a great deal of thought, but if you think your land really needs a push, it's easy to get someone to do it and it isn't even very expensive.

TREES AND SHRUBS

Much of the shaping of your garden can be done with trees and shrubs. These require a moderate investment of money and effort in the first year or two, but what they chiefly need is time. This is one reason why they should be the first plants to concern you. It's true that it is difficult, when you have no experience in garden planning, to decide where you are going to be glad to have a large shade tree thirty years from now; don't think about it that way. You will make mistakes: Your shrubs will be too close together (we all do this); those trees nicely framing your view may end up in front of it. But it's much more likely

Trees, shrubs and ground covers offer easy ways to shape your property, but too often they are used without a coherent plan. Here we'll see how a typical suburban front yard can be made into an inviting outdoor space. You will never garden in a place where you don't want to spend time, so the first step is to establish some privacy and make yourself at home.

that your early trees and shrubs will do well and give you much delight and encouragement. Choose easy, familiar species (more on this later) and plant them well. By the second year, these plants will require almost no attention and you will begin to see the changes they make in the landscape.

Because trees and shrubs require so little care, you can use them at the far reaches of your property, giving your garden something to reach toward as you bring closer areas under control. In your early days of homesteading, you may have too many demands on your time to work on a garden requiring regular attention; think of these early low-maintenance plantings of trees and shrubs as a framework for later, more complex horticultural effort. Of course, these plants are interesting and beautiful in themselves and can bring flowers to parts of your

In this second stage, trees and shrubs form islands to break up the lawn into smaller, more private and more workable areas. A variety of ground covers provides contrasting surfaces; spring flowering bulbs will bloom in these islands with almost no care. At this point maintenance is negligible—go on to more complicated plantings when you have the time.

landscape where you'll never want to exert much effort—the front yard, for example.

The front yard is a difficult area, no matter how it's laid out. In rural areas, many houses are set close to the road; most of the property is behind the house and naturally this is where most outdoor activity takes place. In the suburbs, the opposite is true—here we usually have an enormous expanse of front lawn dotted with specimen trees. The effect is the same, however; no one wants to spend time in front and everything from badminton to barbecue to baby's sandbox is crammed in a small strip to the back. If you have other places in which to garden more strenuously, leave the front to a few shrubs and create your real garden elsewhere. You should make a garden only in places where you want to

Now that your trees and shrubs are thriving, use enclosed spaces and island edges for perennials. Note the absence of foundation plantings; save that area for specimens needing special attention. Toward the road, let some of that lawn break out into a naturalized meadow planting.

spend your time. But if you have no other likely space, you first have to work on making this bare lawn a more inviting place. Build up islands of trees and shrubs which will enclose the property and shut off the road and nearby neighbors (an important consideration if you garden, like most of us, in a uniform of old bathing suits and abandoned pajamas). When you have enough privacy to feel comfortable, more ambitious plantings can be developed out from the edges of these islands. The islands themselves can become tiny woodland glades flowering with native shade lovers and spring bulbs. This is a long-range project, but it makes a good example of the kind of step-by-step development a weekend gardener should follow. You can always just leave it to the trees and shrubs if you find you can't manage more.

As a weekend gardener, you have to keep track of just how much you can do in your limited time. A common mistake is to take on too much at once, then be unable to keep up with your aspirations. Gardening of any kind is a very long-range project. It's best to have an overall view of where your garden is heading (although admittedly most of us, myself especially, don't have this kind of foresight) but don't hesitate to moderate your vision when you actually get down to digging holes. See how your plan can be developed in stages, a bit at a time, while you figure out just how much work you want to do.

Many trees and shrubs occur naturally in clusters; don't just dot single random specimens around your property in the customary suburban manner. Two or three willows by a pond make a much more interesting arrangement than just one; several birch close together can give the effect of a tiny woods. A few fruit trees will become a small orchard. Seating placed near these plantings will make them even more attractive. If outdoor seating is concentrated around the house, many people will venture no farther, but a pretty and comfortable-looking bench placed in the shade at a distance will draw people to it. Herbaceous flowering plants can then, in turn, frame the seat, until the whole area feels like a bower.

Trees and shrubs are, of course, invaluable in dealing with some of the more practical problems of your landscape. This is a country with beautiful views but you may have a neighbor with an auto salvage yard. If this kind of sight is an affront year round, evergreens are the answer; if it's only visible from areas of use during the summer, a wide range of flowering deciduous screens could be used. An effective screen doesn't have to be a solid wall of planting in a line; a looser, staggered arrangement will fill the space just as effectively and create a more natural, pleasant group. Keep this in mind when closing off your own non-garden areas like a sandbox and swing set or tennis court.

SOME MAN-MADE LANDSCAPE ELEMENTS

Planting trees and shrubs is not the only way of shaping outdoor space. Rock walls are an abundant landscape feature in many parts of this country and are a great asset in a garden. The soil of the Northeast produces such a constant supply of rock that you could pave most of your yard with what comes out of your flower beds. Low, freestanding dry walls or retaining walls are easily built, even by a rank beginner (see many of the photographs). Besides shaping the landscape, they form excellent planting sites for rock plants.

America, "the Saudi Arabia of wood," has always made excellent use of this material in country gardens; wonderful old trellises, arbors, enclosed seats, arches and allées are still to be seen in abundance around rural cottages and homes in small towns. With the nonchalance that characterizes old gardens, often these elements just erupt in the middle of a yard, sometimes accompanied by a spectacular vine, sometimes just standing like an enigmatic entrance to nowhere. Much as I love these gardening non sequiturs from another era, I admit they can be used with somewhat more purpose in a coherent design; they have great persuasive power to lure the visitor from one area to another and they make an ideal planting site. Even an amateur builder can construct a sturdy replica at little cost.

Fences are another American forte; from picket to post-and-rail, you can find a fence to suit your garden style. A fence doesn't actually have to enclose anything—just a single section can give strength to a line of planting or direct the eye to a view beyond. A simple fence is often a great help in the early stages of your garden making—it creates an immediate effect for not too much money and if you decide it's in the wrong place, it isn't too hard to move.

PLANTINGS NEAR THE HOUSE: A POLEMIC

In general, the landscape nearest the house is the easiest to control and order; as the garden moves out into the wilderness, it will tend to become more and more wild until it gradually blends into the rest of the landscape. Paradoxically, this should mean that these easily accessible areas near the house are planted last, although this is seldom the case. These more controlled areas are obvious locations for flowers requiring more attention. But the herbaceous flowering parts of your garden are usually the most difficult to figure out and are more demanding once planted. If you can bear to wait a few seasons until you know a bit more about your growing conditions and about the other demands on your time, you'll have a much greater chance of immediate success when you do get started.

You will probably discover that the area immediately around your house is already occupied by planting of a fairly specific sort: foundation plantings. (Be warned that this is a topic about which I have strong personal opinions. I'm making no attempt to be unbiased.) This somewhat recent development in landscape design has been a great setback both to gardening and to architecture since its inception. The original purpose was to conceal the results of bad building, faulty architecture and poor site planning by slapping an assortment of evergreens up against the foundations of a new house. Around a trailer, where they are best employed, they can lend a spurious air of permanence; they can also make a beautiful old country home look like a trailer. These plantings are now an almost universal landscape cliché—homeowners don't plant them because they like the plants; as gardeners find themselves pruning them several times a year, they like them less and less. And most old homes have less than no need of an evergreen fringe around their lower level. Up until the last fifty years, most houses were well placed on the ground with foundations that needed no disguise. Carved-up geometrical shapes of yew or azalea are an insult to the graceful and solid relationship of these houses to the ground. If you have an old house, don't put in this kind of planting; if you're already stuck with it, consider taking it out. This doesn't mean that your house will sit in naked splendor; those foundation areas can be utilized by plants of greater interest and beauty. Since these are the most protected places on your property, they can be used for plants that have difficulty out in the open. If your house does have a foundation that needs covering up, consider a more varied mixture of flowering shrubs interplanted with big perennials, ferns, ground covers or vines. How about draping the entranceway with a rose-covered trellis instead of flanking it with rhododendron? I know it will take more than a few pages of invective to change this unfortunate architectural trend, but as a beginning gardener you could try to see these plantings in a different light. You could have more to your foundation than capitata yew.

Perhaps now you are beginning to get ideas about how your landscape can be shaped to form a setting for flowering plants. Following natural contours and existing features, you can begin to sense how some areas can be enclosed and intimate, some mysterious and inviting, some open and dramatic; how the movement from one place to another is enjoyable and rewarding. All this in one little acre? Keep in mind that these spaces, though often described as "outdoor rooms," aren't really constructed that way, one separate from the other. Often they resemble the spaces within a room—the way a big chair by the bookshelf defines a place very different from the area around the piano, for instance. A large tree or shrub group forms a specific kind of space nearby. A flowering ground cover can set off one place from another, even if they are adjacent. An orchard doesn't enclose an area, but it creates a very specific and inviting atmosphere which can be complemented by naturalized plantings within it.

So far we've really talked only about using trees and shrubs to make your garden. You may be suspecting that all we're doing, in spite of the rhetoric, is making another variation on the low-maintenance suburban plot. I hope, after all our discussion of looking at and thinking about your landscape, that this is not how your design is shaping up. It's important to use trees and shrubs, since these make the overall structure of your design, and it's important to get them going early on. But now let's get on to the flowers. There are many reasons for approaching this part of your garden more slowly. Preparing the soil for perennials is quite a lot of work. Once your perennials are planted, they will require more attention than trees or shrubs. Even after they are established, they can't simply be forgotten or ignored. There is a very wide selection of perennial plants, even for the most difficult climates, and they have, in many cases, more specific demands about their growing conditions than trees or shrubs. You just have a little more to learn about growing things in order to grow perennials successfully. This is one reason why growing them is so interesting, but it's also why you should wait until you have more attention to devote to it. It may not actually take an enormous amount of work, but this part of your garden requires more thought and more understanding of how plants live. The more time you spend looking around you and learning from what you see, the more prepared you will be when you actually get down to planting.

Flowers will provide the sparkle and movement for your overall scheme; they focus attention on certain areas at certain times, and this attention shifts as the season progresses. This is one reason a perennial garden is more interesting than a plot of annuals and one reason not to concentrate your efforts on one big border. Wouldn't you rather have the feeling of seeing flowers around you everywhere you look? Many different flowers can be used in lots of different ways in your garden. Some examples will demonstrate what I mean. Few flowers are more welcome in early spring than the daffodil, and few flowers are easier to grow. Those brilliant splashes of yellow warm the still-bare landscape like sunshine; every year at this time gardeners decide that there's no such thing as too many daffodils. That's a feeling with which I wholeheartedly concur. You can use them in large natural drifts at the very limits of your garden—unlike many spring bulbs, narcissus tempt no browsers. The only care they require is having their foliage left to ripen, which is how the bulb is fed. Herein lies the problem with the way most gardeners grow narcissus. Don't grow daffodils in a mixed perennial planting. The foliage, which is copious in a mature clump, occupies a large space and makes an unattractive yellowing mass well into summer. They don't *need* to be planted in a bed—narcissus will thrive in a well-dug hole sunk in a lawn. And it's wonderful seeing them at a distance—plant some to be seen from the house, to cheer the days when it's still too cold to spend time outdoors. When they are done blooming, let the grass grow up around them as the foliage ages. By this time your attention will have shifted to another part of the garden, and you won't be annoyed all summer waiting for the leaves to die.

The huge Oriental poppies make an explosive transition from spring to early summer; those big heads of vibrant color can provide an accent like nothing else. They are unshakably hardy and easy to grow but they do have a few problems: Their season of bloom is fairly short, especially in areas that warm up quickly in late spring, and they make a huge clump of foliage that gets progressively more unattractive until it disappears, leaving a big space in your border. Like daffodils, poppies don't need to be in a perfectly double-dug bed; send them out on their own into the landscape where they will flourish in spite of weeds and neglect. When they are in bloom, they focus attention like a spotlight on certain areas; when they are finished, cut them down and mow over that area for the rest of the season. (If you can't bring yourself to do that, just mow around the clump as if it were a shrub. It will die off by midsummer). The most familiar and available of these poppies come in shades of shocking orange-red that are not easy to place with other perennials—they are best seen by themselves, against a dark background, or in front of a white shrub like bridal-wreath. This is a timeless country combination, welcome every year. In cool areas, they grow well with the perennial cornflower, *Centaurea montana;* this weedy, pretty plant can be grown with as little care as the poppies; they flower at roughly the same time and make a striking color combination; it's better not to grow either of them in mixed beds because they overrun their neighbors.

There are great numbers of plants that can be used in this way: on their own or in combination with one or two other plants, in large clumps that provide shifting points of color and interest around your garden. There will be areas where you may decide to have small mixed plantings of more sensitive and demanding species but in the beginning, think in terms of big homogeneous bunches of undemanding flowers that can accent the design you are making.

This kind of clump planting is often seen in old country gardens. I've found it recommended in American gardening books from the turn of the century, although it seems to have been out of fashion for some decades. What we find in old gardens today is more likely to be the remnants of somewhat more elaborate borders that weren't kept up; all that remains is a mass of phlox here or there, one enormous *Sedum spectabile,* a gray haze of artemesia around an abandoned foundation. Most of us don't have the nerve simply to plop big plants in the middle of the backyard, however lovely it looks in those old gardens. Start with accent points provided either by your design or by existing landscape features incorporated into that design. It could be something as simple as a mailbox or lamppost, a large rock, the end of a wall, the side or corner of an outbuilding. An isolated planting of shrubs can be amplified with a mass of color that will appear at the same time or provide interest later in the season.

A wall or fence is an obvious location for planting and it provides a wonderful backdrop for a real border. If you're not ready for that yet, don't feel you have to take on the whole length. Establish a few big plants here and there, perhaps with some vines providing interest in between. Don't try to make the masses uniform—have a low, spreading shape in one place, a slender upright spear farther along. As the masses expand—and you won't believe how quickly that happens—you can knit it all into a more cohesive planting.

Too often the space around a house is given over to foundation plantings of lumpy evergreen shrubs with no charm. A wonderful old house like the one above has no need of a foundation coverup.

Prepare the ground for these plants much as you would for a tree or shrub. Dig out a hole twelve to twenty-four inches deep (if you have a plant with enormous roots like the Oriental poppy, you may have to go deeper), break up the subsoil and check for drainage (as explained on pages 16–17). Mix the existing soil with quantities of manure or compost. If the soil is clay, also add sand or peat moss. The overall size of the hole will depend on what you are planting and where you got it. If it's a big clump a neighbor is giving away, make the hold slightly larger than the entire root mass. You may have to divide it several years from now, but it's easier starting with a bigger plant—it will settle in more quickly and you will see right away what it looks like in your garden. If you

Instead, make use of this area by planting vines or old-fashioned flowering shrubs that complement the house and soften its architectural oddities. Clumps of perennials like peonies or iris will also look at home here.

are planting container-grown material, the plants won't be very large now—check books and catalogs to get an idea of the plant's dimensions when full grown. Put three to five plants in the prepared area with generous space between them. It's advisable to use a mulch on surrounding open soil in the beginning while the plants are getting started—this will cut down weeding and watering in the crucial first months. Any open, newly turned soil will quickly be discovered by weeds—one reason not to make the hole any larger than necessary.

You may notice that this soil preparation is not really any easier than that required by a full-scale perennial border. In most ways that's true; there is no real shortcut to soil preparation. It's hard work and it's not terribly interesting but it makes an enormous difference in the success of your plantings. Many of these clump plants we're discussing will survive with quite poor soil, but when you are trying to get them going, it's not worth it to skimp on effort. The plants will settle in and take off much more easily; there's much less risk of failure and having to start over. These easy, fast-growing plants will need almost no attention once they're established; take the time initially to do it right. I am not going into elaborate detail about the actual preparation; it's advisable, if you've never grown anything, to look at a step-by-step planting guide for beginners (see the Bibliography for suggested titles). You'll develop your own procedures with more experience but it's wise to know the essentials.

Aside from the basic, unavoidable, backbreaking part of this preparation, clump planting is an easy way to start using flowering plants. You are dealing with a much more limited area and number of plants than in a traditional border. You are working out the relationships between just two or three kinds of plants. Keep these relationships simple at first: One short mass against a slightly taller one; one that blooms early with another blooming late; if they bloom together, create a simple color harmony or contrast. Even in the early stages of growth, when you have to give your plants more attention, very little weeding will be necessary and that will be easy, since the space is so small and the plants limited. Principal upkeep is mowing around the whole clump with a mower. When bloom is past, cut everything back and direct your attention elsewhere.

Most classic garden perennials require full sun, good soil and good drainage. It's possible that these conditions occur only in small, scattered areas of your property—yet another argument for this kind of modular planting. This will be another factor to consider in deciding where to place your plants. These conditions are not really as limiting as they sound at first. Soil and drainage can be improved in any area, if you work at it (and there are also wonderful plants for damp soil). A great number of good garden plants will do well in less than full sun; in the warmer parts of our country, in fact, almost all flowers do better with a little shade. And there are lovely shade plants you can grow in the really dark corners.

Another great advantage of this kind of planting is that it provides a way of using flowers too ferocious for mixed beds. Over and over you will read about plants that are weedy or invasive. Many of them may be plants you have always loved and have wanted to grow, but they are a disaster when paired with something delicate and slow growing. Some perennials are just difficult to place because of size or color. Some look better by themselves—peonies, for instance: This favorite of old country gardens is usually seen planted in long single lines across a lawn. Odd though this may appear at first, it is a striking way to use this plant, which takes up an enormous amount of bed space and requires no maintenance beyond mowing around it.

It's not uncommon to read garden books that warn against dotting the landscape with little patches of flowers; the usual term of opprobrium for this is "spotty." I think that this usually refers to annual plantings which often look as if they are perched insecurely on the surface of the landscape, never really becoming a part of it. The plants themselves are usually awkward or insignificant—in a large mass they can make some kind of effect, but in small doses they do look pathetic. Your clumps are not going to work that way. These are very bold plants we are talking about—they settle in with an assurance that makes them look as if they've been there forever (when you try to move them you may decide they *are* going to be there forever). And their placement is tied in to elements in the landscape and determined by your overall design. Remember, too, that many of these plants, although they may die back completely in the winter, may be larger than most shrubs; a planting of golden glow may top seven feet and cover several square yards—whatever else you might say about it, you can't call it spotty.

GAINING CONTROL AND LEARNING TO LET GO

These large-scale clumps will enable you to use a lot of flowers around your property; even two or three of these masses blooming in each season will give your whole garden a flowery, country-cottage aura. You will begin learning how to grow perennials at the same time that you are slowly developing your ideas of garden design and bringing your land under control. This control, or lack of it, is an important consideration. It's not unusual in a country property to have nature coming up pretty much to your back door. One aim of your garden design is to push back the frontiers enough to be able to do what you want. Charming though it is to see nature up close, remember that you only have two days a week in which to keep the upper hand. This is the reason to establish mowed areas to keep the meadow out, the reason to have a plan of simple contours that *can* be mowed, and the reason to displace unsightly weeds with flowers that can hold their own with little help. Any hard-to-reach places will immediately fill up with interlopers—animal and vegetable—you don't want. If you can't get in close to the side of the barn, how about a big stand of day lilies instead of the brambles already there? If a muddy low place is a nuisance, a simple planting of lythrum and *Iris pseudacorus* can turn it into a pleasure.

Control is a different kind of problem in the suburban garden. Here you want to be able to free your property from the stultifying rigidity of typical subdivision planting. Clump planting can be helpful here too; use big perennials to replace less interesting shrub plantings, to break up masses of foundation evergreens. Day lilies are the one perennial commonly used in suburban plantings; they are useful and attractive plants but they are far from the only possibility. Vary them with plants of more striking and eccentric personality.

VENTURING INTO MIXED PLANTINGS

When you have both a greater understanding of perennial plants and a greater control of the out-of-doors, you can begin experimenting with more exacting plants and more complicated planting arrangements. I'm still not talking about a border in the usual sense—we have a way to go before we get to that. But there are many plants that you may want to grow which are not suited to our massive clump arrangement. They may be smaller in stature or have a delicate subtlety that is best seen in combination with a few other plants. They may be unable to fight it out with weeds and grass. These plants may still be easy to grow in the right situation but they need slightly more attention. What we will do here is create something similar to a traditional perennial bed but much smaller and more limited in scope. It's always easier to maintain a small space with a limited assortment of plants. You can have more than one of these "planting modules," but in the beginning, keep them separate. As we discussed, there is much to learn about how one plant relates to another; keep these relationships simple while you're first learning how to keep the plants alive.

It may be harder to place these beds in your landscape and for several reasons it might be wise to keep them close to the house. Mixed perennial plantings look best against a solid backdrop of some sort and it's much easier to lay out your plan in two dimensions, like a painting, than in three, like a sculpture. You may read about "island bed plantings" in some books, promoting the idea of a bed you can walk around and see from all sides. It sounds like a nice idea but leave it to experts. It's difficult enough to keep a bed looking good from one or two directions, much less four, and too often these "islands" end up with an undesirable resemblance to the petunia mound or circle of cannas plopped down on the front lawn.

Any wall, fence, line of shrubs or side of a building can form your backdrop. There's no reason not to have a bed up against the back of the house or in a corner by the door—you'll see it, enjoy it and take care of it more often. If there are changes of level to deal with on your property, a series of small terraces provides a perfect planting space for this kind of bed. Each terrace is separate and limited in its selection of plants, but each bears an interesting relationship to the other. You can plant an area in front of a retaining wall; if you're feeling ambitious, plant the wall. When you really become expert, plant a bed at the top of the wall as well. This is an example of how you can slowly knit together these simple units once you have them growing well. If you succeed with a planting on one side of the patio, take on the other. Once your bed fills out along a section of path, try one along the opposite side. Don't feel they have to be symmetrical either in size or content unless you've tied yourself to a very formal structure.

It might be easier to visualize this kind of bed if I give you an example from my own garden. In a small section of raised terrace, the season starts with a simple combination of grape hyacinths and the lovely white daffodil "Thalia." As these are fading, a few of the delicate pink and cream Lady tulips return every year. A cloud of self-sowing forget-me-nots hides the yellowing bulb foliage—when they start to look untidy, I simply pull them all out. Carpeting mats of pink arabis spill over from the rock wall, blooming from April to the end of May. Some small bright pink allium carry on from mid-May through June. At the same time, the rich, dark-red sweet william "Black Beauty" is a perfect foil to penstemon "Elfin Pink," which has an unusual peachy tone. Later in June, miniature scabiosa in pink and lavender surround alpine asters. July brings a host of veronicas. After an easy winter, catanach may return and bloom; otherwise, I put in a few new ones. *Salvia superba* adds an accent of deep purple. *Sedum album* makes a quiet ground cover until it blooms and looks like sprays of baby's breath. Late in the season, *Sedum spectabile* comes to the fore.

This bed is very narrow—fewer than three feet at the widest point—and only six feet long. Because it is raised by retaining walls, small plants are closer to eye level and protected from larger, invasive species; good drainage is also ensured for delicate plants. This bed may not present a perfect floral display every week but there is always something blooming and the bed as a whole offers a series of subtle interplays of color, texture and shape. The grape hyacinths and daffodils *could* be grown somewhere else but seem to work with the other material.

There is a time-honored game played by perennial gardeners called Succession of Bloom. The crowning success in this game is creating a bed for all seasons—the planting unfolds in a continuous array of flowers, all complementing one another and offering bloom from March until November. Need I say, this is hard to do? My feeling is that it's also unnecessary, particularly in a garden with some space. As we saw with our clumps, first one area is in the spotlight, then another. However, if you have a limited space on which to lavish special attention (especially if it's near the house where you see it all the time), you may want to give this problem some thought. I still don't think it's imperative to fill every space with flowers every week of the summer—this would probably require plugging in some annuals unnecessarily—but you don't want this space to go completely dead in mid-July. Aim for two or three species blooming together for each two- to four-week period; some will have long seasons, some short—that's just one of the elements you are learning to juggle.

These mixed beds may be small and limited in scope but they should still use plant masses large enough to have an impact. Never use just one of anything. (The exception to this rule—big shrublike perennials—shouldn't be in this kind of bed.) Plant at least three of a kind, more of slender, upright species like some of the allium.

One crucial part of your garden education is going on as you work in these beds: You are getting more fully acquainted with your local weed population. Don't underestimate the importance of this—it is essential to successful gardening. You've probably gotten to know a few of the really large-scale invaders on your property—burdocks, thistles, teasels—and almost everyone can recognize a dandelion, but until you are offering well-cultivated bed space to the millions, you have no idea of the range of plants that will try to move in. There is an attractive and fascinating handbook prepared by the U.S. Department of Agriculture called *Common Weeds of the United States* (Dover); this is helpful for many of the more obvious and widespread. Unfortunately, there is no real shortcut: You learn your weeds by weeding. At least in a limited group of plants you can have a fairly good idea of what you planted—this is how you start being able to recognize the interlopers before they take over.

Another advantage of small beds is that you can adjust soil conditions to suit specific groups. If your soil is slightly acid, for instance, you can have one special bed for lime lovers like dianthus and lavender; grow your gentians elsewhere. It's not too difficult to change the pH of a small area if you work at it—it becomes vastly more complicated if you are trying to work out all the possible combinations in one bed. The same is true of exposure: If you have a dry, open slope, here is a ready-made location for herbs. Your shade lovers can be accommodated in a little space under an apple tree.

A WORD ON GROUND COVERS

Shade lovers bring us to the subject of ground covers. In the low-maintenance catalog this term seems to be limited to pachysandra, vinca, ajuga and two or three others too boring to remember. These are recommended in areas where a lawn won't grow. But there's no reason to grow something completely without interest when you could use those shady corners for patches of flowers that really require very little more care. Wouldn't you prefer a carpet of violets and lily of the valley to a plot of pachysandra indistinguishable from plastic? We'll discuss this further when we talk about plant selection, but keep it in mind as another easy way to grow certain perennials. Ground covers aren't just for shade, either. Any area that's hard to mow, anyplace where grass won't grow (or even places where it will) can be turned over more profitably to a flowering ground cover. Ground covers don't have to be low, creeping plants that people can walk on. Any plant requiring little attention that can fill an area with attractive flowers and foliage can qualify for this position.

It's nice to grow shade-loving perennials under trees, but don't give in to the suburban obsession for a wall-to-wall carpet of green. There is nothing wrong with patches of dark earth. Few sights are more restful than an unbroken expanse of needles under a stand of pine or moss-dotted ground beneath spreading beeches. When you get around to it, you might want to plant things there, but don't feel you have to fill up space with something you care nothing about.

You now have a number of ways in which to use flowers around your country garden, ranging from the more or less traditional small mixed bed to the somewhat out-of-the-ordinary clump planting. (I must admit that this latter method is only just about to catch on; don't be surprised to find yourself on the cutting edge for a while). There's still another approach that has been increasing in interest recently and it provides a useful program for some tricky parts of your garden.

NATURALIZING AND MEADOW PLANTING

Remember those flocks of golden daffodils? They're not really clump plantings and they're certainly not in beds. This arrangement is usually called naturalizing—the plants are allowed to grow as if they might just have sprung up. Naturalizing often starts from either a clump or a mixed bed—certain species just begin going off on their own. In some cases you may want to encourage this, as when you realize that one species seems bent on taking over your yard. Let it loose on some of the less accessible parts of your garden. Naturalizing can be the best use for plants that look great at a distance, but are too messy for closer study. Naturalizing often suits the "between" areas of your property—among loose groups of shrubs, along hedgerows, at the edge of a wood. It's a good way to use certain plants that don't really fit other categories and it can be an interesting design element, since this naturalized zone can provide a transition from the controlled portions of your landscape to the great beyond. Naturalizing is similar to meadow gardening, but these methods differ somewhat in the plants they use, the area they cover and the way they are established. They are similar in that they provide generous amounts of flowers with little maintenance and they blend the edges of your property with the surrounding landscape. You can, of course, have nothing but a meadow garden if you like—it is well suited to weekend gardening—but it's only really suitable for certain kinds of plants. I personally feel it is more interesting to use as one element among many in a flowering landscape.

Bulbs are most commonly spoken of as being good for naturalizing but many perennials can be used this way, too. Snowdrops, crocus, scilla are all easily planted in the lawn, under trees or around shrubs where they provide welcome early patches of color, then disappear—just take care to let the grass go uncut until the foliage dies. The tiny early cowslip, *Primula vulgaris,* will also flower freely in a lawn. Aquilegia and hesperis (sweet rocket) will thrive in any lightly shaded area, even if it's damp or rocky. They provide a long season of color from spring to early summer. As with your clumps, it's best to grow just one or two species together in a naturalized area. Use big drifts for effect. Lilies are often recommended for naturalizing, but here the choice of species is the determining factor: Big, rampant growers like the familiar tiger lily do well this way or the lovely, wild *Lilium canadense,* but hybrid species will seldom look at home, even if they grow easily. Day lilies are an obvious choice for naturalizing, as you can see on page 216.

In a meadow garden you are attempting to re-create a whole natural environment, a kind of idealized version of the fields around you. Contrary to what you might hope, you can't just walk into a field and sow flower seeds. You are much more likely to succeed if you are starting with no field at all, particularly if you want to establish plants that aren't part of your specific local ecosystem. An area where the soil has been disturbed or deliberately turned will give flowering plants a necessary head start against established grasses. There is a big business now in selling wild-flower mixtures for this kind of planting but you will probably do better collecting seed from species native to your area. Most commercial mixtures have quite a low proportion of flower seeds to grasses, and they often include plants unsuitable to your location. A true meadow is made up mostly of grasses, but you probably want a more intensely flowery meadow than the fields around you. If you plant the flowers, don't worry, the grasses will take care of themselves.

Maintaining your meadow will require mowing once or twice a year, depending on your location and plant selection. The first year or two after planting, hand weeding will be necessary to remove native species like thistles which might be a little too natural for comfort. An extremely thorough and useful book on this topic is *The Wildflower Meadow Book* (Martin, Eastwoods Press). Rosemary Verey's *Classic Garden Design* also offers interesting ideas on the subject.

By this time you could have a large repertoire of plants flourishing in various ways around your property. Clearly, some approaches are better suited to some landscapes than others. A few landscapes may have one or two dominant features demanding specific treatment, like a water garden or rock garden. (Some of these possibilities are discussed in Chapter 7.) Your own limitations of time and energy are foremost among the determining factors; that is why I cannot repeat too often: Start slowly. As soon as it starts to get out of hand, you may feel overwhelmed and you might lose interest. Better you should feel calmly confident and nonchalant about your success—then it's time to take on more.

AND YOU STILL WANT A PERENNIAL BORDER?

It's possible, even after your clumps are the envy of all your neighbors, that you still have a longing for a classic perennial border. Well, if you really want it, you should be ready to make the attempt. It's mostly a matter of putting together all you've learned from your smaller modular plantings. By now, you should have some idea of attractive color combinations. You probably have a pretty good sense of the size and effect of quite a few plants. You're beginning to understand your soil conditions and how to vary them. You're getting to know your local weeds and how to deal with them. And you now have a better understanding of the landscape as a whole and of your design in relation to it. The trees and shrubs are assuming some stature, making your design more confident and developed. You will have a better sense of how to place your border to best effect.

Do keep in mind, however, that a perennial border really does have to be *big* to be effective. This is the problem with almost all the attempts commonly seen in small gardens: They don't use enough plants and they don't have enough space. Often the topography of your property simply doesn't offer this kind of broad, flat, well-drained expanse of ground. Even if it does, a perennial border is by far the most labor-intensive way to bring flowers into your garden. However, if you really want to do it . . .

Don't abandon the other kinds of plantings you've established—the smaller beds will still be useful for trying new species before you use them in a larger collection. You will find that plants often have to be moved around until you find the setting that suits them best: A promising candidate for a clump turns out to need more attention—use it for the back of your border. A low edging turns out to be determined to take over everything in sight—a new ground cover is discovered.

Even with everything you've learned, you may find that a big border is just too much work. Don't hesitate to give it up if it's occupying too much of your weekend. Go back to more big clumps or turn the space over to shrubs. There may be a time a few years from now when you can manage it more easily. Remember, you still want time on the weekend to sleep late, take long walks, swim, play tennis, make great meals and do nothing. A weekend garden should let you do any or all of these things, and more.

3
. . .
FINDING
YOUR FLOWERS

ou may not have worked out every detail of your master plan, but perhaps now you are beginning to get a sense of your property as a series of spaces and masses, and you are probably furiously impatient to start planting. Those abstract spaces marked "tree," "shrub" or "clump" need to be realized by something green and alive; all you have to do is figure out what to plant.

A good basic plan is essential to the creation of any garden and it is important to have a design that can be developed slowly, in pieces, if it is to be utilized by a gardener with limited time. But plant selection is the point at which a weekend garden succeeds or fails. Plant selection is the difference between a nicely laid-out garden so nondescript you don't even notice it and a tiny pocket garden that always seems to have something worth a look. It's the difference between a landscape full of flowers in spite of the proprietor's numerous tennis games and social engagements and a fussy collection of plants that's a nonstop pain in the neck.

You may already be thumbing through garden catalogs in search of your plants and building up a library of gardening texts; all that will be useful, in time. For now, look closer to home. Two basic "rules" for plant selection are: First, grow what everyone else is growing; second, grow what no one else is growing.

GARDENING WITH EVERYONE ELSE'S PLANTS

My first recommendation may be such a letdown that you are now hurriedly skipping pages to go on to the second. I'll try to explain quickly. We're returning to my initial exhortation to look at everything around you. At first all you may see are petunias and marigolds—try to go beyond that. Look in early spring, before tender greenhouse plants arrive to confuse the scene. Bulb plantings will first get your attention, then the spring riot of flowering fruit trees and shrubs. They may be followed by such old garden classics as Oriental poppies, iris, perennial bachelor buttons, *Cerastium tomentosum,* creeping phlox, lemon day lilies, bleeding heart, various kinds of primulas—these will all be up and blooming in most areas before the end of May, when garden-center flats are just beginning to be set out. Even through June you can be pretty sure if you see something large and permanent-looking in full bloom, it's likely to be a hardy perennial. Some of these plants have made their way into suburban consciousness, but you are much more likely to see them around older houses in small towns or farther out in areas where traces of agricultural life still linger.

There may not be American cottage gardens like the English models that inspired Gertrude Jekyll, but there are people out there growing flowers, flowers that "just come up" and have done so for years. Sometimes these plants are the toughest, most persistent remnants of a garden planted when perennial gardening was more a part of life than it is today. Often the arrangement of these flowers is nonchalant in the extreme—it would probably not occur to you that these are gardens. They're not, really, but they can provide you with information (and inspiration) for your own cottage garden.

You may insist that in your area no such idealized rural models exist. You just don't know how to look—you're probably imagining something much too pretty. My particular part of the country is a far cry from the immaculate landscape and picturebook towns that prevail in many rural parts of the Northeast. Trailers of astonishing colors are more common than center-hall colonials, and many of the once fine houses are clothed in siding that can make you wince. With this kind of setting, it's easy to overlook a trellis of clematis or a stand of madonna lilies that would break the heart of a serious gardener. Less than half a mile down the road from my farm, one neighbor has amassed a collection of debris which fills completely the quarter acre around his house: farm machinery, kitchen appliances, tools, cars, furniture and objects I've never identified. In the midst of this wreckage a large stand of lemon day lilies bursts forth each spring, closely followed by two enormous bright pink peonies. A majestic mock orange perfumes the scene in June. No one in his right mind would call it a garden, and there's a strong urge to look the other way that may overcome the plant hunter. Across the street an elderly woman lives in a house the size of a studio apartment, surrounded by land that could be covered by a tablecloth—there is less than five feet between the house and the road. She always has something in bloom, yet she's so seldom doing anything to her flowers that for several years I thought the house was abandoned. Early wild plum accompanies daffodils; a huge bleeding heart dominates the scene in May, while hesperis springs up around the woodpile; Oriental poppies, aquilegia and iris take over later, followed by a climbing rose. For a few years one vivid blue delphinium amazed me, although this year she told me that "they just didn't come back so easy." She thought it might be a blue hollyhock. Hollyhocks of somewhat more ordinary but still lovely colors carry on until phlox and golden glow arrive to finish the summer. These all spring up out of the grass—when they start to look finished she levels them with a lawn mower.

None of these plants is anything exotic or breathtaking in itself (although the delphinium was something of a shock), but taken together they create that wonder of gardening books: succession of bloom. You may not want to imitate the way in which the plants are used, though in some cases you may see a

It may not look like a garden, but you can learn a lot from flowers you find growing in a yard like the one above. This is where you can see which hardy plants survive neglect, which species thrive in your specific gardening conditions. These plants will make up the backbone of your weekend garden—and they'll look even better without the truck tire.

combination or arrangement worth re-creating. Local plantings like this are helpful mostly to establish a group of plants that will survive. The hollyhocks may have rust and the iris borers. They bloom anyway. These are the kind of plants you're looking for.

These perennials will provide the backbone for your garden—they ensure that if all else fails, something will still be in bloom. These plants survive in your climate. You may not yet have discovered the depths of your winter temperatures and frost dates may still be a mystery, but if the little old lady down the street can grow hollyhocks and bleeding heart, you can too.

You probably won't know what most of these plants are. This is where your books and catalogs can help, although many worthy old-fashioned perennials seem beneath the notice of plant sellers. You may also notice, once you've managed to track something down, a huge discrepancy between the plant you've seen growing and the one pictured and described in a book. The habits of plants vary widely—another good reason for seeing a plant growing before choosing it for your garden.

WHAT WAS THAT PLANT?

If you want to know what a plant is, stop at a garden and ask. This is extremely helpful in some ways and not so helpful in others. The gardener probably won't know what the plant is—her sister had a piece of it from a neighbor of theirs who brought it back from somewhere. Or he thought some people called it upside-down flower or fairy bells but he isn't sure; it's always been here since he's had the place. This may seem somewhat beside the point but don't let your urban impatience take over. The best way to learn about gardening is from other gardeners, especially if they are years ahead of you in dealing with a difficult climate. Many rural gardeners may not be learned—they don't speak Latin and don't know the pH of their soil. They've learned to garden by observing how things grow and any of this you can learn from them is an enormous help. Gardeners, for the most part, *like* other gardeners and enjoy talking gardening. They also enjoy sharing gardening—most gardeners of my experience are incredibly generous with their plants. (I could have doubled the size of my garden with all the plants I was offered in the course of working on this book.) Don't be surprised if you end up going home with a piece of that plant you stopped to ask about. You may never come to know its name, but it will have a permanent place in your garden.

It's always helpful to your general garden awareness to visit any kind of public or private display garden, botanical garden or arboretum, but this sort of planting can lead you astray on the question of plant selection. Places of this kind, if they do feature perennial plants as well as the usual bedding annuals, can offer you an opportunity to see species you've only read about in books and can give you ideas about how certain plants look in conjunction with others. One thing you won't know is how easy such plants are to grow. Plantings of heaths and heathers always look irresistible to me when I see them in some botanical collection—low mounds of glowing tapestry colors like a miniature medieval landscape. Without careful attention to soil and growing conditions, and skillful pruning at the proper times, these plants become miserable untidy lumps. Stately eight-foot delphiniums will fill you with awe and envy and you can scarcely be blamed for longing to try them, but no one ever said they were easy. These display gardens, even in days of horticultural cutbacks, have a staff to serve their plants in a way no weekender can aspire to. Enjoy these gardens, and learn from them. But you still may be better off copying your neighbor down the street, especially if you've never seen him working in his garden.

SELECTING TREES AND SHRUBS

These will be the first plants you need to obtain, since they arrange the setting for the rest of the garden. In many ways they are the easiest plants to select as well, since in most parts of the United States their numbers are limited. Besides noting the plants used around homes in your area, take a look in the local cemetery or churchyard, often excellent places to see fine, fully grown specimens of trees and shrubs. Although these places are maintained to some extent, seldom are the larger plants clipped or forced into artificial shapes and little effort is made at spraying or fertilizing them. In our area, the cemeteries boast the loveliest tree hydrangeas; farther south I've seen churchyards accented with majestic clumps of huge ornamental grasses. Old shrub roses, now lost to commerce, can often be found here. Seeing mature plants like these gives you a far clearer sense of how you might use the same species in your garden.

The best way to acquire good trees and shrubs for your garden is to locate a well-established nursery in your area that grows the plants it sells. Many highway garden centers are no more than truck stops selling plants grown all over the country. Often the sales help will have no idea whether a plant will live in your area. There is usually no guarantee for the health of the plant. These garden centers can be useful sources of inexpensive plant material once you know what you're looking for and once you know how to recognize a healthy plant. In the beginning, find a reputable local operation. They will know how to deal with your climate. They will usually offer some form of replacement guarantee for the health of their material. It's not necessary that all their material be grown locally, but if they have raised even part of their selection, they have a pretty good idea of how a range of plants performs in your area. This, combined with some kind of guarantee for the health of the plant, may make them very scrupulous about selling plants with a borderline chance of survival. My own local nursery sells many things to me with extreme reluctance, since I live fifteen miles west and several hundred feet higher than their location. They consider this the equivalent of sending their offspring into Siberia and occasionally refuse to believe I can keep certain specimens alive. This infuriating attitude has saved me a great deal of money and effort. Such a nursery is probably selling the plants that you have been seeing in everyone else's yard, and this is to your advantage. Use the planting vernacular of your area to establish your overall design. Local plants will give your garden the look of the surrounding landscape, the feeling that your garden has been here forever. The selection may seem limited—all the better. You don't need a wide range of species for this stage of your garden—you are much better off with large numbers of a few different kinds.

If you are in the suburbs or in a fairly affluent community, your local source could have too much to offer. The catalogs of plants might reflect recent vogues by landscape architects for exotic specimen trees and bizarre shrubs. Later, possibly, you may find a way to use them. For now, avoid fancy foliage types. Variegated plants, especially, require real skill in placement. Dwarf conifers are enormously appealing but difficult to place in a natural country milieu. Don't buy a weeping anything unless you have a specific use in mind (willows are an exception). You may feel that you're getting left with only boring plants: arborvitae, barberry, juniper, lilac, mock orange, spiraea, hawthorn, crab apple, cherry, magnolia, forsythia—a much longer list could be made of these dependable old favorites. They're *not* boring, although some have been misused in contemporary plantings. They're familiar, because they've had a place in the country garden for the last hundred years. They may not all be spectacular, which means that elements in your design won't call undue attention to themselves, and they're successful, which means that you can plant them and forget about them. They will continue to flourish while you go on to more fascinating subjects.

NURSERY SHOPPING FOR BEGINNERS

Most nurseries offer plant material in three ways: bare-root, balled and bagged (B&B), and in containers; in some ways these conditions may limit the size or variety of material you acquire. Container-grown material, both woody and herbaceous, is usually easiest for weekend gardeners, since the plant can happily remain in its pot until you get a chance to plant it. Plants are available in containers year round, which relieves some of the frantic spring rush to plant everything at once. For these reasons container growing has revolutionized the nursery business in the past decade. One great drawback is that only plants of a fairly limited size are available this way. Another disadvantage is that these plants are usually more expensive than alternatives. For a really large shrub or tree, a field-grown plant will have to be chosen—this is dug up and its root ball wrapped in burlap (balled and bagged). Although a plant can remain in this state for a limited period of time—and, in fact, you will frequently see trees sitting in a nursery lot for sale this way—it should be planted as soon as possible. Even small shrubs sold this way are amazingly heavy and hard to manage—large trees are better delivered and planted by professionals. Nice though it is to have some large trees and shrubs put in, in most cases it's easier and usually much cheaper to select smaller plants you can handle yourself. If you are buying and planting a large number of plants—say, a hedge or a collection of fruit trees—bare-root plants should be considered. Plants are available this way only in early spring, when they are still dormant. When you go to buy them you really must know what you're after, because these frozen sticks certainly don't resemble anything you want in your garden. They have the great advantages of being quite inexpensive and easy to transport, handle and plant, and in a few weeks they will surprise you by looking almost as good as container-grown plants costing much more. They do require immediate attention, however; a whole spring weekend should be set aside for this project. Since you can get an entire orchard in the back of your subcompact, be sure bare-root buying doesn't get you into a classic weekend garden bind—picking up more than you can plant. Your whole landscape doesn't have to be planted this spring.

There should be a place in your design for both deciduous and evergreen material. In the North, evergreen trees and shrubs are limited mostly to conifers: pine, spruce, fir, hemlock, the wide variety of juniper species, yew and arborvitae. These evergreens are in the spotlight through the winter—in many northern regions that could be November to late April, so don't underrate the importance of these plants. With them you can create a landscape that becomes apparent only after the leaves fall. Farther south, broadleaf evergreens become more and more dominant; in parts of the Deep South, Florida and California, these plants provide so much of the domestic landscape year round that gardeners must remind themselves to plant deciduous material to vary their design and offer seasonal contrast.

Select trees and shrubs with more than just one season of interest. Shade trees will have an important place in your design but they don't have to be nondescript—use a few with beautiful flowers, such as aesculus (horse chestnut), catalpa or paulownia. Berberis may not be your favorite hedge plant but it has fine autumn color and carries its vivid berries all winter long. Liquidambar and *Euonymus alatus* share the traits of spectacular autumn color and sculptural winter beauty.

Vary also the rate of development for different parts of your scheme. Plant some trees for quick, temporary growth, even if they are short-lived. A Lombardy poplar may live only twenty years in many parts of the United States, but will make a spectacular exclamation point in the landscape in just two years. In twenty years you will have other well-grown, more permanent specimens in the garden to replace it. Willows will quickly provide a large soft mass in your landscape but you don't want to use them near your house—the roots invade your plumbing while the branches litter your lawn or break your roof. Plant them and enjoy them at a distance—near your pond, for instance—and wait for a slow-growing, well-behaved tree like the European linden to provide shade near your home.

Fruit trees are an easy way to add a flowering season to your garden and most local sources will probably have a wide selection (the suburbs in particular are well endowed in this area). The range of just crab apples alone is enough to confuse any tree shopper. Flowers are important, but keep in mind that many varieties have beautiful and varied fruit that will add interest into winter, and several have attractive bronze foliage as well. Don't, however, confine your interest to apples. Plums provide much earlier flowers, sparsely arranged along black twigs. Cherries, pears, peaches, almonds all extend the season in one direction or another, depending on what your climate dictates. Try not to focus on the fruit as a crop—that can get you into the necessities of spraying. Consider that any fruit is an unexpected bonus.

In many places dwarf fruit trees are offered for sale. Usually these are stunted-looking, awkward creatures and have no place in a country garden. If a small tree is preferred for a certain location, *Malus* "Red Jade" is a small, slow-growing crab apple with a gently weeping shape and brilliant, tiny red apples in fall. The English hawthorns, varieties of *Crataegus laevigata,* are equally valuable small trees, blooming slightly later than the apples. These hawthorns look like ancient specimens after less than ten years of growth and they are spectacular in bloom.

The range of shrubs—flowering or otherwise, evergreen or deciduous—varies greatly from one area of the United States to another; in mild and hot regions, there is a huge selection available and these plants will contribute much more to your garden here than in the North. Many classic herbaceous plants don't perform well through the unpleasant southern summers and their place as the focus of the garden is often taken by semitropical shrubs that bloom practically year round. There are, as in all things, numerous trade-offs: Mild regions with no true winter don't experience the spectacular and moving change spring brings to the dead land every year, and familiar, beautiful flowering shrubs of the North appear confused and ineffectual in southern regions, blooming sporadically at the wrong times as if trying by trial and error to find spring again. Southern natives and semitropical plants may not have the same kind of overwhelming brilliance in bloom, but the extended season provides something in flower all the time.

Because of the large number of available shrubs in warmer areas, it's all too easy to end up with a yard like a patchwork quilt. Especially at first, limit your selection: Use larger numbers of fewer plants. Don't put your shrubs in competition with one another—when the azaleas are in flower, for example, a more subtle plant is bound to be overlooked in spite of its charm. Arrange a sequence in which just one or two plants have center stage at one time.

In the North, shrub selection is much more limited and somewhat easier, but the same suggestions are helpful. Shrubs can be especially useful in extending the flowering season before (and sometimes after) that of herbaceous plants. We are all most familiar with spring-flowering shrubs, but keep in mind that there are less well-known species that can amplify the range of garden plants through the other seasons. Potentillas are a somewhat confusing group of species, since some are hardy perennials and some small shrubs. The shrubby cinquefoils, as they're called, resemble small roses (to which they're related) and bloom for a long period in summer. Tamarisk and cotinus are two summer-flowering bushes with attractive foliage as well; the purple-leaf smoke bush, *Cotinus coggygria,* is one of the most beautiful foliage plants, with its rich red-bronze color. There are a few other trees and shrubs with leaves in this color range and these, unlike the variegated or "golden" varieties, are an extremely effective contrast in the landscape. Purple plum, *Rosa rubrifolia* and several varieties of crab apple and maple all share this trait.

Don't underestimate the value of fall color, from flowers, foliage or fruit. The tree hydrangea is a star of the fall: Its enormous heads of bloom harmonize with all the rich autumn tones—ivory, peach, russet and gold. Native witch hazels are not often considered desirable garden plants but they can be placed unobtrusively at the edge of a wood—in October or November they will suddenly grab attention with their delicious fruity fragrance and odd golden flowers that linger for over a month. There are Chinese species of hamamelis that flower in milder areas in January. Fruit or berries are a great asset at the end of the season—often they stay on a tree or shrub for months, providing interest into the winter. *Ilex verticulata,* cornus, elaegnus species, viburnum, the shrub roses, mountain ash, bittersweet, the innumerable hawthorns and crabs, the ferocious, thorny barberries all create a whole new kind of garden until hard-pressed birds and animals take their toll.

We're all prepared to accept that most trees and shrubs (except the tropical varieties) have a fairly short blooming period. What we tend to forget is that we have to live with the plant for the rest of the year. The look of a bush out of bloom should be almost more important a consideration than its flowers. Don't give star billing to a performer who looks great for two weeks and boring for fifty. I consider lilacs indispensable in the country garden but if mildew drives you crazy, plant them away from the main focus of the garden. Enjoy them in May, then forget them.

Local nurseries usually offer nonnative plant material. To some extent this is because most people want their garden to look different from the rest of the landscape; it's not really a judgment on the value of particular species. Where local species are for sale, don't hesitate to use them. You could go dig one up from another part of your property but that kind of transplanting is a risky business until you have more experience. It's better to spend the money to get something that will live. Beautiful native *Amelanchier canadensis* has become a more popular tree in commerce recently, and with good reason. It combines early flowering and a graceful, small stature with extreme hardiness—a perfect country-garden tree whether it is native to your region or not. It's commonly called shadblow, since it blooms when the shad are running in the Hudson River. In California and the Southwest there are numerous species of native ceanothus and arctostaphylos which should have greater use—it's surprising to find them recommended more often in English gardening books than in American ones.

Your local conservation department or agricultural extension agency could be an unexpected source of information on plants. These people are obviously experts on climate and growing conditions in your area and often have suggestions for planting material for specific problems—trees and shrubs to prevent erosion, for example, or plants to attract and feed game animals and birds. If you have wooded acreage, they can furnish experts to assess your property for its forestry potential and set up a program by which existing woods can be managed and improved. Many conservation departments sell—very inexpensively—recommended plant material. The plants are usually tiny and bare root and may come in quantities overwhelming to a weekender—we actually planted 1,000 four-inch-tall larch trees one weekend years ago; almost all of them survived and now many are over twenty feet tall. This may not be the most convenient way to buy plants but it's well worth looking into.

You can save yourself a lot of gardening time in the future by careful consideration during plant selection. Pick a plant to fit the situation in which you want to use it. It's true that pruning and careful management can enable you to keep a big plant small or a leggy shrub compact—for a while, at least. But this will require time and attention. If you give the question careful thought ahead of time, you can almost always come up with a plant the natural size and shape of which will suit your location. Big, vigorous shrubs should be used out in the open where their size isn't a concern—their pruning can then simply be a matter of your convenience. If you try to place them in a confined area, be prepared to be cutting back several times a year. Any kind of formal, shaped hedge presents the same problem. If you have the space, a loose grouping of trees or shrubs will provide an effective screen that needn't be fussed over. If you don't have the space, a fence might be a better solution.

THE ROSE QUESTION

Besides the standard trees and shrubs, your local nursery may offer a few other categories of plants. One likely possibility we may as well attack head on: roses. Almost everyone wants to grow roses, and almost every plant place sells them. I asked my usually scrupulous plantsman how people in our Zone 4 climate could hope to grow hybrid tea varieties. "Well," he replied, "come winter, you dig a pit three feet deep . . ." I stopped him at that point. I can't imagine growing anything that requires digging a pit three feet deep every winter. In areas where the climate is milder, the disease and insect problems are worse. You *can* grow hybrid tea roses in a weekend garden; my father, the ultimate weekend gardener, has over one hundred varieties and a flower border as well. But you really have to be devoted to the idea, and it is much more work than I would ever want to spend on the weekend.

You don't have to give up on the rose completely. Not all roses are hybrid teas. Other rose species may not have that classic rose look, but they don't have the salient drawbacks either. The great race of roses includes—and, indeed, developed from—a large number of independent, once-wild species, and some of these species can still be bought and enjoyed in the garden without much work. The rugosa roses, originally from Japan, are a widely available group of this kind and a good example. These are mostly no longer true species roses, since many hybrid forms of rugosa are available, but they are easy and they make excellent landscape material, something that can never be said about hybrid teas. The hybrid teas (I'm including floribundas, etc., in this category) are really grown only for the flower. The bushes, even when kept free of their eternal plagues, never look natural, which is reasonable, considering how hard it is to keep them alive. They can best be used all together in one mass bed, which by its nature calls for a fairly formal layout. In short, these roses don't work in a weekend country garden. The shrub roses, on the other hand, act like shrubs, making generous masses of interesting and attractive foliage that look good throughout the season and often providing hips for fall color as well. It's probably best to think of them first as shrubs, second as roses, since often they don't really look much like roses. *Rosa harisonii,* Harison's yellow, is a true old-garden favorite found all over our country, especially in severe climates; it has tiny leaves and small flowers of a particularly lovely pale gold, blooming from mid-May to the end of June. *Rosa rubrifolia, R. macrantha, R. gallica officinalis, R. wichuraiana*—there are literally hundreds of these lovely species, some more available than others, some hardier than others, almost all easier to grow than hybrid teas. In the Midwest especially, efforts have been made to produce even hardier hybrid shrubs that perform well in extremes of heat and cold; it's worth the effort to seek them out.

Some of these fine shrub roses may be available locally but most will have to be sought through mail-order catalogs. Roses are probably the best material to buy mail order—their size and root structure are well suited to bare-root transport, so don't hesitate on that account. Your local nursery may offer a selection of "hardy climbers" like "Blaze" or "Golden Showers." Like the shrubs, these bloom only once but for a fairly long season; they are generally carefree where they are hardy.

VINES TO CLIMB, HANG OR SPRAWL

Climbers lead us to another broad category: vines. These are a little difficult to discuss generally, since some are annual, some perennial, some tender, some woody and some even evergreen. They are united in our discussion by a characteristic lax form that requires either another plant or a man-made structure to give it support. Because of this requirement, placement must be carefully planned—you can't just sink a clematis in the ground and wait for results. But this is also a group of enormous value in the country garden—these are plants that can make your trailer look like a Tudor cottage (well, almost), your fences and arbors as if they've been here always. Vines can add another layer of bloom to trees and hedges. They are plants for pulling things together, for blurring the edges of new gardens and making them feel settled, complete. Don't be in a hurry to use them out in the landscape until you find suitable places for them; use them around the house while you wait. Consider replacing dull foundation plantings with arbors of clematis. Screen one side of your porch in a thick green curtain of Dutchman's pipe—this a classic country convention. Your lamppost or mailbox could be swathed in garlands of everlasting pea. Hardy flowering vines likely to be found through local sources are clematis, trumpet vine (campsis), honeysuckle, wisteria, climbing hydrangea, euonymus, Boston ivy and Virginia creeper (*Parthenocissus* species). In warmer climates the range broadens far beyond the ubiquitous bougainvillea—jasmine, tropaeolum, lantana, plumbago, ficus or passionflower. Climate dramatically alters the habits of many of these vines. In our area trumpet vine is well behaved, even timid, yet it is listed in *Weeds of the United States* for its invasiveness farther south.

FARTHER AFIELD: IN SEARCH OF PERENNIALS

Local sources may offer other old garden favorites: tall bearded iris, peonies, Oriental poppies. But don't be surprised if your nursery doesn't have a wide selection of perennials. For these we may have to do more specialized shopping. You may be lucky enough to find someone in your area who sells plants in a more or less informal manner. Usually this is a gardener who began by selling extra plants for which he or she had no space. Sometimes a simple sign announcing "Plants for Sale" is all the advertising you may see for the establishment. Near us, one wonderful gardener uses her spectacular plantings of creeping phlox to stop traffic in early spring; when you look more closely, you can spot boxes of newly dug plants for sale. In some cases this informal approach has developed into a more organized business with a catalog, definite hours and set prices. What this kind of source has to offer is, usually, a chance to see plants growing in a garden; an opportunity to acquire a large, well-grown specimen; and the advantage of talking with someone who is growing the plant who can tell you what it is and how to grow it.

Often the only way you can hear of these places is through other gardeners, another good reason to get to know people in your area with this interest. One source of information could be a local arboretum or botanical garden, however small. Often places like these will have periodic plant sales to raise money—this might give you a chance to meet other gardeners and share information.

It is unfortunate that in some areas local garden clubs have a primarily social rather than horticultural orientation—most serious gardeners wouldn't come within a mile of them. This might be unfair to many of these organizations—consider sounding out one in your area to see if it has anything to offer.

Other gardeners are, without doubt, the best help in selecting and acquiring plants for your garden, particularly for those large-scale clumps we talked about. Most gardeners are only too glad to be rid of a chunk of something big and fast-growing. Offer to divide the iris or day lilies of an elderly neighbor—this will guarantee you enough plants to carpet your yard. If development threatens to raze old houses for a road or shopping center, see if you can get in ahead of the bulldozer and remove any plants worth taking. (We raced ahead of our new interstate, digging up scores of ancient peonies which now grow peacefully in our yard.)

With a little detective work, some luck and a bit of charm, you can probably acquire enough plants locally for at least the backbone of your garden. These plants will mostly be old garden favorites and they got to be that way because they are easy to grow, undemanding and hardy in your climate—primary qualifications for weekend garden plants. Even if you don't manage to acquire the plants themselves, you will at least have developed ideas about which species you want to grow if you can find them. Then it is time to start looking through your collection of mail-order catalogs.

HOW TO READ A GARDEN CATALOG

It takes little more than the purchase of a trowel or pruning shears to become a name on a garden-catalog mailing list, so you may have received a selection of catalogs by now. If you haven't, the gardening page of the Sunday paper usually has ads for several. Garden and outdoor magazines will have advertisements. If you have access to the library of a horticultural society or botanical garden, you can usually find a huge selection. A local garden club may have a collection. Ask other gardeners which ones they receive.

Once you have an assortment that is as mouth-watering as it is confusing, learn how to use it. Keep in mind the basic plant categories we discussed earlier—annual, biennial, perennial, woody shrub or tree. Remember the terms hardy, half-hardy and tender. Keep zone numbers in mind. By now you should have some idea of what zone you live in. Some catalogs are scrupulous about listing the zone for every plant; many ignore the problem. Try to deal with firms that give you as much cultural information as possible. Try to buy plants from sources with a climate equal to or worse than your own—this doesn't always guarantee hardiness but it helps. Limit your orders until you know the quality of the plants you receive. Do the plants appear healthy? Are they the size advertised? Does the firm replace plants quickly if you have a complaint?

All these catalogs are uniformly misleading on the question of season of bloom. Were their descriptions correct, all plants would maintain a constant level of flower production from April to October. This hyperbole may be to some degree unintentional, and not meant as hyperbole at all. It is very hard to be precise about when a plant will bloom, even in a specific area, and the blooming period varies widely from one region to another. There are general rules for figuring this out: Every five degrees latitude north delays flowering about three weeks, for instance, but you would have to know the original point from which to figure. Even these methods are extremely inexact, since northern areas are later with early flowers but somewhere about July start getting earlier with later flowers. Sound confusing? All this doesn't usually matter unless you are bent on creating very specific planting combinations and working out a rigidly exact sequence of bloom. You would be well advised to abandon those ambitions for now. It's fascinating and inspiring to see brilliant plant combinations in other gardens but there are lots of reasons they may not work for you. I preen myself every year at the wonderful (and completely accidental) conjunction of *Allium aflatunense* and *Camassia quamash*—both perfect weekend garden plants; the starry spears of silver blue camassia make a foil for the precise purple globes of allium. In my father's garden they bloom several weeks apart. In a friend's garden one won't bloom at all, no explanation given. In another part of my garden the camassias are about eight inches tall, not the three feet they are next to the allium.

To return to the original point, catalog descriptions of plants blooming from April to October usually mean that somewhere in the United States this plant starts to flower in April. In others it probably blooms in June. (English gardening books add to the confusion because many perennials grown in Britain's cool climate have much longer periods of bloom.) There are very few plants that literally flower all summer, although some, if cut back regularly, will often produce later bloom. In northern areas, cool-weather perennials like aquilegia or lupines may keep flowering through July. In the South they're over in May. Don't feel discouraged by all this—it gets much easier to figure out when you're growing the plants. But now, perhaps, you see the importance of starting with flowers you've seen blooming in your neighborhood.

As we discussed with shrub selection, the appearance of a plant when it's not flowering is a consideration (this is one reason I like to visit gardens in April or November—I really enjoy the look of the plants themselves without the distractions of flowers). All beginning gardeners are absorbed in the flower question—how big, how many, for how long. Keep in mind that perennial plants are very different from annuals, where the flowers are the only concern. The dramatic foliage spikes of yucca, huge felt-leaved rosettes of verbascum, silvery blue mounds of dianthus—these have as much character as any plant in flower and these will make up your garden year round.

An extended period of bloom is a desirable asset but don't overlook some choice plants because they perform for two weeks only. The Siberian iris gets short shrift from garden books on this account. It's true they bloom for only a few weeks and like all the iris, when they're over, they're over. But they come at a particularly desirable time, just before most of the big perennials get going, in that little pause between spring and summer. Few plants are easier to grow. Out of bloom they provide striking clumps of graceful foliage and seed pods. If you grow them in a border they probably take up too much space. If you have them in clumps on their own or naturalized around a pond or swampy area, they are a real asset for no effort.

When I first started buying plants, I wanted the biggest, toughest, most indestructible ones I could find. The words "weedy and invasive" immediately got my attention; "needs plenty of room" was music to my ears. Space is usually what you've got in a country garden; time and energy are what you're short of. Plants that would overwhelm a border can have a place at the wilder limits of your property. These hardy giants may be a nuisance to you later on (although you can always dig up big chunks to pass on to someone else) but my personal preference is for plants, however weedy, that won't die.

It's easy to acquire a large number of perennials that flower from the end of May until the beginning of July—these are the most widely available herbaceous plants. Once you have those set, start expanding your flowering season. The flowers that bloom very early and very late often have an impact that is greater than the huge variety of blossom available in midseason. Tiny iris and snowdrops in February or March are so welcome that every year I promise myself more for this time of year. This is one reason rock-garden plants have so much to offer—they provide a whole season of bloom before the rest of the garden is barely awake. As the leaves turn and fall, I'm easily enchanted by the vibrant contrast of our native New England aster and its hybrid forms. The sudden appearance of sternbergia or autumn crocus is an unexpected delight.

There are numerous hazards in buying mail-order plants. Some plants can survive for a week or more with their roots lightly wrapped in peat moss. For others this is a disaster, no matter how carefully they are handled. Some plants are shipped in containers—this is better for some plants but can be very expensive. (If a catalog does not specify container shipping, you should assume your plants are traveling bare root.) Some growers solve this by selling very small plants. Often this is a worthwhile way to buy perennials; the plants are inexpensive and some species that can't be moved in maturity can be moved only at this stage of growth. The plants often don't make much of a show the first season and it is usually best to plant them in a holding bed until they can fend for themselves in the rest of the garden. Bare-root purchases, although larger and more expensive, also sometimes need a year to recover—you may be better off with the smaller selections.

There is one large group of plants about which I've said nothing so far: bulbs. I haven't referred to them separately in earlier chapters because in most ways they can be considered as a modified form of perennial, and like other perennials they can be either hardy or not, invasive or not, easily grown or not. The bulb is actually a highly specialized formation of the stem used for food storage. During dormant periods bulbs are easily handled, making them ideal subjects for mail-order purchase—you will find lots of catalogs devoted to them. In many ways most bulbs make perfect weekend garden plants. Many of them are planted in the fall, when there are few conflicting garden activities; once planted, they can be ignored until next spring or summer, when they bloom, usually without fail. They don't require much undue fussing or attention; some of them multiply at a reasonable rate; they can provide bloom earlier and later than ordinary perennials; and many of them are very inexpensive. After that kind of sales pitch, you may wonder why everyone doesn't grow more bulbs, something I wonder myself all the time. I can only suppose that many gardeners are led astray by tulips. Tulips are beautiful flowers and I think I'm safe in assuming that most of us love them, but they're not great garden plants for weekenders. They don't really come back successfully after two or three years. They have the disadvantage of all bulb plants: You must leave the unattractive yellowing foliage to mature and feed the bulb. Unlike the daffodils, however, they don't lend themselves to naturalizing, where the foliage problem is not so noticeable. The standard cottage or Darwin tulips are quite formal-looking flowers and aren't really at their best in informal clumps. And everything eats them—mice, rabbits, woodchucks, deer. Perhaps beginning gardeners assume all these problems accompany all bulbs; if this is true, let's make an effort to spread the word: Other bulbs are easy. Awe-inspiring lilies look like prima donnas but for the most part they aren't. In cold climates, you could have different species of allium blooming from May through September. In warm locales freesia and ranunculus start practically midwinter. Crocus can delight you in earliest spring, then surprise you with species blooming in November.

Most bulbs require good drainage, as do the rest of your perennial plants, although some, like *Allium moly* or *Fritillaria meleagris,* flourish in big clumps in damp clay. Some require a very dry period for summer dormancy, making them a perfect choice in hot, arid regions. Like perennials, some are extremely hardy and some are tender, for example gladiolus. The familiar gladiolus may be another reason new gardeners are suspicious of bulbs— they are practically impossible to use in a garden. They are tempting for beginners because they are very inexpensive and reliably produce enormous and colorful flowers, but they always look awkward and artificial coming out of the ground. If you have a vegetable garden, stick in a row to use as cut flowers.

There are other tender bulbs frequently offered by catalogs: Some, like sparaxis, ixia or crinum, can be left in the ground in the South or California, where they perform like perennials. Some, like tritonia (usually sold as montbretia), are advertised as tender but surprisingly come back anyway even in Zone 4—they're worth planting even for one season of bloom, since they are inexpensive and require literally no care after planting.

The vast race of allium contains such favorites of mine they've received two pages of photos (130–31). If you begin to suspect after looking at the pictures that I'm really just talking about onions, you're right. Onions, garlic, chives, leeks all belong to this family, and all unite the virtues of beautiful flowers with few demands on your time. The stately, spectacular *Allium giganteum* is probably the most widely offered—unfortunately, it is not the easiest to grow and usually doesn't return after one or two years; when you see what can be achieved with the much more accommodating leek or *A. christophii,* you might decide not to bother with the giant. *Allium moly, A. sphaerocephalum, A. caeruleum, A. ostrowskianum* are all well represented in most bulb catalogs; many other species can easily be grown from seed. A few, like *A. neapolitanum,* are not quite as hardy as others but most survive the greatest extremes of either heat or cold. Most, not surprisingly, smell like onions, but this would be a ridiculous reason for not growing them.

Don't be intimidated by the beauty of the lily—there is no reason not to plant these spectacular bulbs in a weekend garden. Lilies need good soil and good drainage, like most perennials; they prefer full sun in cool climates, some shade in warmer zones. You may have seen big stands of the classic orange tiger lily, *Lilium tigrinum,* around old houses—these are among the easiest to start with. They are best in clumps by themselves, first because they multiply rapidly, second because their peculiar tone of orange is difficult to place. Most of the other species and varieties are better grown among mixed perennials. The glorious trumpet hybrids have a scent as overwhelming as their size and colors—no July border should be without a few. Rubrum lilies may be the last word in elegance from your florist, but these plants don't act as if they know it; they provide a much-needed high point in August and September. The one recurrent problem all the lilies share is susceptibility to late freezing—keep winter mulches on as long as possible. Unlike most perennials, lilies will not recover from a hard freeze—all growth and flowers will be lost for the year.

Some bulbs requiring winter dormancy may not flourish in the warmer parts of our country, but with plants like agapanthus or alstroemeria available, fussier species will scarcely be missed. Mediterranean and South African species should be sought out here—these flourish *because* of summer drought, not in spite of it. Western natives like calochortus, fritillaria and brodiaea further extend the selection for favored parts of California and the South.

WHY CAN'T I GROW THIS PLANT?

I've scarcely begun to enumerate the bulbs you can grow in your weekend garden—start going through your catalogs now. So far we've filled your garden with trees and shrubs from local nurseries, hardy perennials from special growers or the gardener across the street, shrub roses and bulbs from a wealth of mail-order catalogs. These plants are already more than enough to fill up a garden—you may have noticed that happening already. Not all are going to succeed for you—this is a sad fact you must face sooner or later. Plants are living organisms and their requirements are not always easily known, even by people who have been growing flowers for years. In the beginning you will make simple, often silly mistakes—not knowing basil isn't hardy; trying to grow gypsophila and gentians together. You will also have beginner's luck—spectacular lilies you can't believe, a vibrant haze of Chinese delphinium through October. You will, invariably, try to take on too much and some things will suffer, just because you can't keep track of it all. Later on, as you garden with increasing expertise, you may be surprised and annoyed to discover there are still plants you can't grow. Sometimes it's you, sometimes it's them—there *are* plants, and many of them, that are hard to grow for a variety of reasons. I call them primadonna plants. They may be wonderfully tempting and someday you may have the time, but for now, forget it: Don't waste your weekend fussing over one flower. Get the rest of your landscape established, get lots of easy perennials flourishing—you can work on the difficult subjects later.

Occasionally some plant that should be perfectly easy gives you a hard time. It may be that you are overlooking some ovbious requirement, like enough sun or water. But there are times when a plant everyone else is growing won't grow for you—this is one of the mysteries and heartbreaks of gardening. Forget about it for a few years, then give it another try, but don't be surprised if it still doesn't work. Luckily, there are more than enough other plants to grow.

WILD FLOWERS—YES OR NO?

As you survey the countryside, looking for possible plant material, it's unavoidable that another whole world of plants should catch your eye: wild flowers. Here are all these plants growing happily in your climate without a bit of effort on the part of anyone. Aren't these perfect candidates for the weekend garden?

Well, this a good question, but not an easy one to answer. All our garden plants at one point or another developed from wild plants and there is no reason to believe that the resources have been exhausted. The only problem is that you have to know quite a bit about plants and gardening to make wild flowers work for you. A great many of them are either too easy or too hard. The ones that are too easy we call weeds; the ones that are too hard we call lots of things, prima donnas being the most polite. It can help your gardening a great deal to learn about your local wild flowers, since they can offer clues about your climate and growing conditions—you can learn which kinds of plant respond to acid soil, which can grow out of a sheer rock face. Many of the loveliest of these have produced garden hybrids that you can be fairly certain will survive in your locale. Many of the most familiar roadside weeds were originally brought here as garden plants, like day lilies, Queen Anne's lace and Japanese knotweed—these are referred to as "aliens" or "escapes." Some of these, if they can be controlled, might be useful in the wilder parts of your landscape, but if you take in something like polygonum, you are courting disaster. It's not only the alien invaders that behave in this fashion, of course; goldenrod, much loved though it is in European gardens, can be a real pest on home ground. At the other end of the scale are some of our loveliest native plants—ravishing in the wild, languishing in the garden.

In between are some wonderful and easy additions to your plant list: *Monarda didyma, Asclepias tuberosa, Lobelia cardinalis,* caltha (marsh marigolds), aquilegia, *Aster novi-belgii,* trillium, the western sunflowers—these are a small sample. All of these are available in commerce—this is a useful clue about a plant's garden worth. In many cases—asters, for instance—numerous hybrids have been produced. This doesn't mean that these are the only wild plants that will grow easily and well; it's merely a starting point.

If you recognize that a local plant, native or otherwise, is weedy and invasive but still beautiful, use it in naturalized areas at the limits of your property. Some wild plants, while not necessarily weedy, require a large expanse to display their value—buttercups are an example. A meadow garden is a good solution in this case. Should your weed turn out to be less pushy than you thought, give it a try in more select company.

When handled with caution, some of the prettier weeds of your area can contribute to your plant collection. It's not surprising to find that often these flowers are more highly esteemed away from their native place: The lovely musk mallow, *Malva moschata,* is a carefully tended perennial in Long Island, while upstate gardeners casually pull it out of their beds. I take great pride in my vibrant clumps of *Asclepias tuberosa,* the brilliant orange butterfly weed; you almost never see this beautiful plant in gardens farther south, where it is native.

If you want to grow a local plant, even a weedy one, don't dig it up in the wild. Many of our best wild flowers are, of necessity, protected plants: It's against the law to dig them up from the wild. Many of them, as I have said, are available commercially. Some may be growing on your own property or that of someone who will give you permission to move it. It's best, whenever possible, to collect seed and start from scratch. This is not always easy, but it protects the plant in its natural setting. When you grow it at home, try to replicate this setting as much as possible—sunlight or shade, rich soil or poor, dry or damp. Even with careful attention of this sort, your wild ones may not make it. Don't be disappointed—you're just not ready to expand the range of ornamental horticulture. As you garden more, you'll develop a better sense of which of these lovely plants you can utilize and which you can keep alive. Until then, look for them and enjoy them where they are.

In some of the most difficult climate areas of our country, the native plants of the region may be your best bets in the garden. Up in the rugged mountains of the West or in the severity of the southwestern deserts, familiar garden plants are going to be at odds with both the growing conditions and the look of the landscape. But the indigenous flowers of these areas feature specialized adaptive mechanisms—this usually means that they not only grow easily in places where ordinary garden flowers expire, but that these plants look more at home in the landscape. In climates like these, let native plants teach you how to make a garden.

ANNUALS—FILLING THE GAPS

I haven't really forgotten about annuals. As I've said before, American gardens are all too often made up *only* of annuals—what I want to do in this book is restructure our gardening habits by establishing the place of perennials and hardy bulbs. Those plants will guarantee a weekend garden of flowers every year, even with minimal effort. Annuals can then be given a suitable place for the changes they provide. They can often extend the season of your garden— many perennials bloom well in spring and early summer but give up in mid-summer temperatures. Annuals can then take over to finish the season with a colorful flourish. In the South and West, where gardens carry on practically year round, annuals are indispensable for filling in gaps and carrying on when perennials go dormant. They also appear more at home in that climate and setting.

Decorum is a difficult concept to discuss in a general way, since our decisions on this question are shaped by strong personal taste. Gardening decorum consists of using plants that are suitable for your setting and the style of your garden. Some of this is determined by a plant's behavior in a climate: Many tender annuals aren't suitable for northern gardens because they don't grow very well there and they never look as if they're growing very well. But even when they do grow well, many of them persist in looking out of place. Our view of them is shaped by years of seeing formal public plantings, bad re-creations of Victorian "bedding out." They can be used to effect in a mass but when seen next to a hardy perennial planting they just look all wrong. Geraniums are a good example: They can be wonderful in big pots or window boxes; when planted in the ground they look uncomfortable and hopelessly artificial. "Wax" begonias live up to their name—molded lumps of implausible material.

Vibrant salvia is a hot spot in the landscape, impossible to place with more subtle and interesting plants. Now, none of these plants is a true annual—they are all tender perennials grown in greenhouses until they are "bedded out." In climates where they can live year round they assume a more natural personality. The closer a plant is to its natural growing conditions, the easier it is to grow and to use in the garden. Some plants, of course, will always have an awkward shape, even when perfectly at home. Some plants (like those wax begonias) never look quite real. But there are hardy annuals you can use to effect in your weekend garden, once you know what they are and how to manage them.

Some hardy annuals are available in flats from garden centers, and you may want to start your experimentation this way rather than trying to grow your own plants from seed. Good annuals for country gardens include cosmos, larkspur, calendula, cleome, nicotiana, annual dianthus, annual phlox. Some western specialties include clarkia, godetia, nemophila, collinsia.

It is traditionally recommended that annuals be used among perennials in the classic mixed border. I hope I've talked you out of that border but even in small mixed plantings annuals have a hard time. A common early-spring mistake is sticking small annual plants in the spaces between the perennials. Every year you will underestimate the speed and vigor with which the older plants take off. The annuals are crowded out before they even begin to settle. It's more manageable to have beds of early bulbs which are then filled with annuals for later flowering. Most annuals are shallow rooted and can be planted without deep digging, which might endanger the bulbs below. The annuals will be filling out and starting to bloom as the bulb foliage withers.

Annuals often need more attention than perennials: They are more easily overrun by weeds, their shallow roots often require more frequent watering and they must be picked to prevent them from going to seed. For this reason, besides the nuisance of having to plant them, it's best to plant just a few each year. When your garden is first getting started and the perennials are still small, you will probably want to use quite a few annuals to fill up your beds, but after that, you really won't need them.

Some hardy annuals, if they find themselves at home in your garden, will seed themselves and return the next year. This, in most circumstances, is devoutly to be wished. Often they will grow much more vigorously in places they choose for themselves. They may not come up where you planted them— they may not come up where you wanted them. But once they start this pattern they no longer really qualify as annuals, requiring extra care and attention. Self-sowing annuals then join your hardiest perennials in being part of the permanent flowering fabric of your garden.

Biennials can operate in this fashion, too, and it is really the only reasonable way to grow them. Familiar old garden flowers in this category include foxgloves, sweet william, lunaria, hesperis and verbascum; they are frequently sold as either annuals or perennials, which makes it all confusing. Biennials grow the first year, flower the next, then die. If you want them in your garden you have to be planting them every year, like annuals without the instant gratification. If they start to self-sow, however, they will establish a schedule by which they are more or less permanent. Most of these plants do have a great tendency to sow seed—all you have to do is allow the seed heads to mature and keep track of the seedlings when they appear, lest you pull them out.

All this talk of seed may remind you of a big pile of catalogs we haven't mentioned: seed catalogs. Some weekend gardeners assume that growing flowers from seed is time-consuming, difficult and usually unsuccessful, and this view is supported by books which make it sound more like a complicated series of laboratory procedures than a part of gardening. It's really just like everything else—some plants are difficult from seed, some easy. Some of the easiest flowers from seed can't be obtained any other way—the delightful annual poppies are good examples. If you want great numbers of plants, seed is obviously the way to get them. Often, in the first stages of your garden, it's easier to buy plants. If you can find a good selection of material, this is the best way to start. But once you've established a framework of easy plants, you may very likely get the urge to grow things nobody else is growing, to plant flowers you've never seen. You are becoming a confident gardener and know better how to handle both your growing conditions and your time. There are a great many more good garden plants out there than you've been able to find through the usual sources and just about the only way to grow these plants is from seed. It's time to go on to the next stage of gardening and the next chapter: the basics of propagation.

4

. . .

PROPAGATION

I usually skip the chapter on propagation when I'm reading a gardening book—now that I'm writing one, I feel the same temptation. It never really seems as if the fun of gardening is to be found on the propagation benches or in the nursery beds. Besides that, propagation requires time and attention to detail—few of us have much of either to spare on weekends.

In the last chapter I enumerated various ways plants could be acquired without an understanding of terms like layering, root cuttings or division. It's easier to start a garden with big plants, usually the bigger the better. And once you've filled at least part of your landscape with flowers everybody can grow, you may be perfectly happy to leave it at that. But I doubt it. A delightful garden with excellent succession of bloom can be provided by thirty or fifty species of flowering trees and shrubs, bulbs, perennials and a few hardy annuals. This may seem like a huge number but getting to this point takes little more effort than you would spend growing a far more limited number of annuals or vegetables. In fact, once these hardy plants are established, you may begin to feel that they really are not a great deal of trouble after all; even a few more perennials could be easily added by the weekend gardener. This is the point at which "gardener" begins to take precedence over "weekend"; this is when you have to start to grow your own.

There are still a few shortcuts available before getting involved in the real business of propagation. The first is getting the plants to do it for you. The second is getting someone else to do it for you. Only as a last resort need you do everything yourself.

LETTING YOUR PLANTS DO IT

Left to themselves, your plants will start to reproduce. This isn't surprising, since that's what flowers are there for, although most species are also carrying on less obvious and more surefire forms of reproduction than sex. Taking advantage of your plants' natural urges will not, in most cases, get you different plants but it can certainly get you more.

Most perennial plants can be divided; after several years, most perennial plants will *have* to be divided. You don't have to wait until it's necessary; if you have a specimen that is growing well and you are madly eager to have more, dig it up. The size and arrangement of roots and crowns will dictate how to proceed. Big clumps often consist of many independent but interwoven crowns (the growing point above the ground, the junction of root and stem). These crowns can be separated from one another into plants of whatever size you wish. Larger clumps will resettle more easily, bloom more quickly; smaller clumps will give you more plants. Some plants grow as a big rosette of leaves— wait until baby rosettes are produced around the edges of the main plant. Some species like pulsatilla make two or three crowns with thonglike roots wrapped around one another—these are hard to divide but it can be done: Immerse the entire plant in a bucket of water and slowly unwind the roots from one another. Plants with a single deep taproot should not be divided: asclepias, gypsophila, baptisia, dictamnus or hellebore are examples. Some plants make large mats which thrust down roots from the stems when they touch the ground—small sections with roots can be cut off from the main plant and moved elsewhere. Some plants have underground runners—new plants start appearing several inches or several feet away from the parent; these are all available for starting in new beds.

In general, spring-blooming plants are divided in fall, fall bloomers in spring, but a lot depends on your weather patterns. If you have a cool August and damp fall, this is a good time to proceed. If fall brings heat and dry weather, early winter may provide a better time in mild areas. Newly divided plants need almost constant moisture until the roots get reestablished. A light cover from direct sunlight can cut down water loss. Large, leafy plants moved late in the season should be cut back on top. Because of the special requirements of newly divided plants, it's often more convenient to set up a nursery bed where more attention can be given to them. This bed can be away from the "public" parts of the garden, in light shade or under a lath shelter, and used for all kinds of propagation procedures, as well as for resting new bare-root purchases.

Bulbs have their own versions of asexual reproduction. Large bulbs will slowly produce smaller bulbs around them—these can be dug up in the fall, when they are dormant, and separated. Some lilies also produce bulbils along the stem at the leaf nodes. These look like miniature bulbs, and they can be used that way. It will be several years before a bulbil produces a flowering plant, but it's certainly not much effort to pick them off and stick them in a nursery bed out of the way. A few years from now you will be astonished to find a blooming clump you had forgotten all about.

What about bigger, woody plants? Most of us wouldn't have the nerve to dig up a big shrub and try to divide it, but frequently new shoots from the ground can be removed with a section of root and replanted. Lilacs are readily multiplied in this way; lonicera, mock orange and spiraea are other old-garden favorites with this habit of growth. Keep in mind that grafted hybrids like French lilacs will produce suckers of the common rootstock, *not* the hybrids.

LAYERING AND CUTTING:
MORE PLANTS FOR MORE WORK

Layering usually sounds complicated in books, but it is still a method of reproduction in which the plant does most of the work. Layering works best for
plants with a natural tendency to run along the ground, but more upright specimens with arching branches can still be tried. You want to encourage the plant
to form roots where the stem touches the ground. The best candidates are
strong year-old shoots, and the time to start is early spring. Make a shallow cut
along the underside of the twig, then peg that section of shoot securely to the
ground. The soil should be fine, loose and rich in humus. Firm the soil around
and over the layered section and water well. Best results occur when the soil is
kept constantly moist—not always a possibility for a weekender unless you
have an automatic watering system. On the other hand, you've nothing to lose.
Check periodically to see if any rooting is started but don't be in a hurry—this
method is often used for shrubs that are slow and difficult to reproduce by any
method. If good root growth has occurred by autumn, you can sever the branch
from the parent but don't move the new plant until next spring. The carpeting
junipers frequently layer themselves this way—if they don't, a little encouragement will get them started. Cotoneaster is an excellent subject. Forsythia layers
best from the tip of the arching branches. Clematis can be stretched along the
ground and layered in a serpentine—one bud below ground, one bud above.

All forms of layering and division will eventually produce plants exactly
like the original parent. As you can see, it's not really a lot of work for the
gardener. Cuttings are another way of multiplying plants which can't be divided
or which don't set viable seed. It's more work than layering and the results are
haphazard for weekenders who don't pay close attention, but it's worth a try.
This method is used most often with shrubs or trees, although perennials can
be grown this way, too. Pieces of stem two to four inches in length are cut from
this year's growth—wood that is young but fairly hard. Snip off the leaves along

the lower portion of the twig, leaving two or three sets at the top. Rooting hormones are simple to use and helpful in controlling fungus. Dip the stem in hormone, then insert in a container of sand and peat. Cuttings must be kept constantly moist and in high humidity while roots start to form. Some plants respond to this method with gratifying ease—willows, for instance. The shrub roses and their relatives can also be propagated this way with little trouble. Remember, though, that most roses are grafted onto hardier roots to survive cold climates—your cuttings will be growing on their own roots and may not make it.

Root cuttings can be used to propagate certain species with brittle roots like anemones, or fine roots, like campanulas. Pieces of root two to three inches long are cut and buried in sandy soil. Be sure the root is right side up and that the upper tip is just under the soil surface. These, too, must be kept constantly moist until growth commences.

Cuttings are a particularly easy way to obtain plants from other people. Even generous gardeners may not be prepared to dig up their plants for you, but few will refuse to offer "slips" from something you admire. Cuttings are usually taken in summer, but are chiefly dictated by the growth of the plant. Don't take cuttings just before flowering, or when a plant is in bloom.

GOING TO SEED

Besides the varieties of asexual reproduction, your perennials will also be producing seed. Most gardening books are strongly against allowing perennials to go to seed—that very phrase has become one of opprobrium. If you are growing special hybrid forms or colors, it's likely that seedling plants won't preserve those characteristics. A case much pointed to is that of phlox, because many "serious" gardeners resent the familiar mauve-colored flowers that frequently result from phlox group sex. (Many special hybrids won't produce viable seed, so often this isn't even a problem.) But a great number of our nicest perennials are just plain species, and seedlings will not veer too far from the original. We discussed self-sowing a bit when we mentioned annuals—it works the same way with perennials. Simply let the seed mature and fall. If you want to take extra care, spread the ripe seeds in a cold frame or nursery bed. It's easiest, though, to let nature take over. Just keep an eye out for seedlings when they appear.

I believe that chance seedlings enormously enhance the look of a country garden. The hardest thing for most new gardeners to do is to loosen up. If you carefully manage a neat, confined little selection of plants, it's very difficult for the garden to develop a life and spirit of its own. It doesn't really begin to look like part of the landscape until you free your hand. Self-sowing is a wonderful aid to letting go. New plants start appearing in inconceivable places and look right. Combinations spring up that never would have occurred to you. Plants find growing conditions which suit them better than their original location. You can eventually get tired of this kind of gardening free-for-all, at which time it's easy enough to start cutting off seed heads again. But up to a certain point self-sowing can add a great deal to the whole outlook of your garden and it certainly can produce a lot of plants for no work. One way in which self-sowing frees your gardening style is by providing more than enough plants for reckless experimentation. You can find new and extreme ways of using your plants once you have plenty to spare. There are ways to encourage seeding—if I have a bare patch of ground I'd like to fill, I spread handfuls of seed heads over the ground and leave them there. The old stems and capsule debris form a loose mulch for tiny seedlings when they start to come up. This is an effective way to cover steep bare patches in need of ground cover—thyme and dianthus will speedily take over when encouraged in this manner; crown vetch can go from a few plants to a whole mountainside with this kind of help.

Now, not all perennial plants will self-sow. Some species need special conditions to produce seed, or don't produce seed that is viable. Some plants require very precise circumstances for seed germination—a cycle of freezing and thawing, or certain daytime and nighttime temperatures. These requirements could drive you crazy if you were trying to control the germination your-self—surprisingly, when the plant is left to its natural pattern, these require-ments are often more easily met. At least you don't have to feel responsible.

Sometimes the seedling plants are not as vigorous as their parents, or have less attractive colors or form. Remember that to a great degree horticulture con-sists of selecting choice plants out of the multitude—be prepared to do likewise. Most of these new plants will replicate their parents, more or less, but occa-sionally you may get a real surprise. Sports are sometimes produced—seedlings that are wide departures from the original plants. Close species in a genus will frequently intermarry, with results that may not be great additions to plant sci-ence, but are fascinating for the gardener. The short, plump, vivid-blue Japanese aquilegia in my garden has gotten hopelessly involved with other species, pro-ducing very tall, very blue flowers that bloom extremely late. The perennial yellow foxglove, *Digitalis grandiflora,* crosses with its white biennial Turkish cousin to create a beautiful peach-colored hybrid that is hardy and perennial. These examples are far from unique—they won't occur in every batch of seed-lings, but they crop up often enough to make me very cautious about disposing of new plants. And they are all the more delightful for being completely fortuitous.

GOING TO SEED CATALOGS

Leaving such good fortune aside, division, layering and self-sowing will pro-duce more of the plants you've already got; to expand the range of your garden beyond the familiar and easily obtainable, you'll have to start new species from seed.

Even the most mundane seed catalog makes enthralling reading in mid-January, but it's really not easy to know what to buy. Many of these catalogs seem more concerned with getting you to buy seeds than getting you to grow them. The selection is usually heavily weighted in favor of tender annuals—

One easy way to deal with plant propagation is to let tough, invasive species take off on their own out in the landscape. Then wildly spreading root runners or ferocious self-sowers are no longer a problem; they're an asset. A large stock of plant material will make it easier to colonize the farther reaches of your property. Note how clumps highlight landscape features, either natural or man-made.

three pages of marigolds, for example, and one entry for oenothera. Zone numbers appear sporadically. Germination time is a closely guarded secret until you receive the package of seed. This is an important point: The longer a seed takes to germinate, the greater the chances of something going wrong. There are some wonderful plants that take six months to two years to germinate, but I'm not interested. There are catalogs that offer both a wide and wonderful array of species and lots of cultural information up front, where you can use it to make your selection. These are the people from whom to buy your seeds.

GOING TO GREENHOUSES

You may still be able to get out of starting the seeds yourself. There are probably small greenhouse operations in your area which grow the familiar assortment of indoor plants and tender annuals. Often these growers can be persuaded to start flats of perennials using your seeds. In a well-managed greenhouse setup, it's not much more trouble to start something a little different. Perennial seedlings will often be smaller and take longer to reach transplanting size, but they don't really require a great deal more work. Some growers may be happy to expand their selection of plants at no financial risk and it's in everyone's interest to have an ever-increasing selection of perennials for sale. I split the number of germinated seedlings with the excellent local greenhouse I use. This will still result in a much greater number of plants than you have need of at a much lower cost than if you bought plants. And of course you have the wild excitement of growing something you know nothing about. I'm not exaggerating. When you first start your garden, you will be delighted with anything that will grow for you. As you become more successful, you may become more and more amazed at the number and variety of plants there are that you can grow, no matter what your climate. The urge to grow new plants waxes stronger each spring. Of course, as you venture farther afield in search of new material, you must expect more frequent disappointment. There are easy and wonderful plants that few gardeners are growing, but some plants aren't grown because they're hard to grow. They may be easy to germinate and *still* be hard to grow—gentians and meconopsis are good examples. (I love to think of one great rock gardener recounting the demise of a hundred gentian seedlings. "Oh," she said, "when I think of the plant material that has marched through this place!") If your garden is made up mostly of easy perennial material, a few setbacks may be disappointing, but they'll scarcely be noticeable. Just go on to something else.

STARTING YOUR OWN

You may not be lucky enough to find someone to start your seeds for you. It's still worth some effort to start them yourself, although the results may be somewhat more haphazard. The easiest way to go about this is with a cold frame or seedling bed—any small separate area away from the main garden can be used. A raised bed is helpful because weeds can be easily controlled, work with the tiny seedlings is more convenient when you don't have to bend, and seed is less likely to be carried away in an early spring flood. The soil doesn't have to be deeply dug, but it should be well drained. A fine mixture of sand and loam is ideal. Seed can be sown in late fall or early spring—many hardy perennials need a freeze to break dormancy. Sow seed in straight rows so you can recognize the plants from the weeds. Most seed should be lightly covered and the soil then firmed over it; a few plants, e.g., digitalis, must have light to germinate, so don't cover them.

Different seeds respond to different temperature combinations—you'll probably get a flush of tiny seedlings in the earliest days of spring, when cool-weather plants like poppies, linum or delphinium get started. When the temperature rises to mid-sixties, many more will appear: Anemone, anthemis, coreopsis, gerbera, lupine, primula, ranunculus are just a few. The bed should be kept lightly shaded and moist—seedlings suffer easily from heat and drought.

Even fairly cavalier treatment of your seeds will result in a surprising number of plants for little effort. Keep the bed well weeded—since it's a small space, this isn't much trouble. When seedlings start getting crowded, gently thin the rows and begin moving the larger plants into a nursery bed. Annuals can be moved directly to areas where they'll bloom. A few perennials such as baptisia or dictamnus can be moved only when very small—they can be set in their final location now as well.

Transplanting requires quite a bit of care and you might be tempted to skip it by sowing perennials directly in mixed beds. If you already have perennials growing in those beds, this usually won't work. It's too easy for tiny seedlings to be overlooked among larger plants and their self-sown progeny. The ordinary garden chores of weeding, cultivating and mulching all endanger your seeds. If you have them scattered all over your garden it's inevitable that you'll lose track of what was planted where, even if you label assiduously. A few plants may survive but the odds are against it. A small seedling bed will produce many more plants for little more effort.

LET'S NOT START SEEDS EARLY

What about starting seed early indoors? Now you're really asking for a lot more trouble. Most gardening books and seed packages seem written with the assumption that you'll start your seeds this way. The advantages are that annuals started early will bloom for a longer season; some perennials and biennials will bloom the first year. The disadvantages are dozens of little containers of sterilized soil all over your house which have to be cared for all the time. Watering, feeding, light and dark all should be carefully controlled. If you need cold to break dormancy, you have to fill your freezer with these things. I find peat moss in the ice cubes for months afterward. If you have a neat shelf arrangement of timed plant lights and a heating cable, it's somewhat easier but still a nuisance. Fungus diseases will spring up and wipe out entire flats in a few days. You can't go away between February and May unless you have a competent plant sitter. I probably don't have to describe in detail the fascination these little packages of wet soil have for small children and pets—the results can be easily imagined.

At some point in your gardening life you will probably want to do this, and you may actually have success. (For all my complaints, I did get some plants out of the mess.) But most weekend gardeners might be better content with nature's efforts in their behalf.

FARTHER OFF THE GARDEN PATH:
IN SEARCH OF THE WEIRD AND WONDERFUL

Once you develop special interests in your garden, you will find that the standard seed catalogs are quickly exhausted. Surprisingly few of the best rock-garden plants are available through commercial channels. Many beautiful native plants can't be found in the usual sources, in spite of increasing interest in their use in gardens. If you develop a liking for penstemons, for instance, you may be puzzled by their unavailability, in spite of the huge number of beautiful plants in this genus. Or it might just be that you want to grow a few really out-of-the-way plants. Depending on your specialty, you can probably find a society devoted to it. There are groups for penstemon lovers, iris growers, day lily fanciers, bromeliad fans and aficionados of cacti and succulents, to name just a few of the better known. These can usually be located through a botanical garden, general horticultural society, agricultural extension agency or garden club. Most of these offer newsletters or magazines and often sponsor some form of plant exchange or seed list. The magazines will usually have ads for nurseries or growers specializing in their area of interest. The seed-exchange programs can bring unheard-of plants within your reach. It's a complete gamble, of course. The American Rock Garden Society, for example, has a seed list of more than 5,000 entries, including every kind of plant from alpine miniatures to giant sequoias. It's really just a list, too; merely a Latin name and a number. This is my yearly version of playing the lottery, since I never know if I'll get what I want, or if I can grow it. But that's the fun and excitement of it; even with my nonchalant methods there are a few successes each year: brilliant pink and yellow mimulus that turn out to be hardy; a tiny soft-tangerine poppy; a huge oenothera with flowers the size of saucers, opening like searchlights at dusk each night.

These special societies also have membership directories to help you to locate other gardeners sharing your taste in plants. You can start your own plant- and seed-exchange programs. Here again propagation is a useful tool— it can provide you with extra plants for barter or for gifts.

There is more to propagation than this chapter takes on, but I'll leave such topics as grafting and air layering to those of you with world enough and time. You probably know enough now to produce all the plants you want. Remember, let the plants do as much as they can. Don't be paralyzed by a fear of failure— greater gardeners than you have sacrificed untold numbers of seedlings in pursuit of something new and wonderful to grow. Be prepared to face death with equanimity. On the other hand, don't waste time over prima-donna plants. There are always a few choice species that seem worth extra time and effort, but if after a few attempts you're getting no results, go on to something else.

Be prepared to discover that you just don't like some of your latest conquests; they may not turn out to be worthwhile garden material, or they may not have a place with the rest of your plants. It's interesting to discover that a native cactus will live in Zone 4, but don't feel you *have* to grow it just for that reason—I, for one, can't stand to look at it.

You may find that these new projects are keeping you from the rest of the garden. The well-established areas and easier plants will need less attention than your latest acquisitions, but don't let the garden suffer overall while you pursue the newest species of saxifrage. Remember your original naive pleasure in growing the simplest flowers in everybody's garden and don't let your exuberant cottage plot turn into an obsessive collection of oddities. Keep your enjoyment of the garden as a whole, as the setting of your home in the landscape. There's more to a garden than the plants.

5

PESTS, PETS, POISONS AND PLAGUES

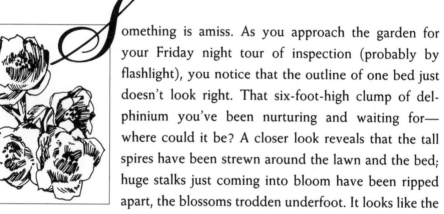

Something is amiss. As you approach the garden for your Friday night tour of inspection (probably by flashlight), you notice that the outline of one bed just doesn't look right. That six-foot-high clump of delphinium you've been nurturing and waiting for—where could it be? A closer look reveals that the tall spires have been strewn around the lawn and the bed; huge stalks just coming into bloom have been ripped apart, the blossoms trodden underfoot. It looks like the work not of a mere madman acting at random, but some maniac who hates all of nature and you and delphiniums in particular. Whoever thought that gardening was just a pastime for peace-loving flower children? As you stand by your wrecked plants, shaking with fury and screaming revenge, you realize that this isn't just gardening—this is war.

Does this seem overstated to you? If it does, you haven't yet had your first encounter with a woodchuck. Or deer, rabbit, chipmunk, mole, raccoon, squirrel . . . the list is impressively long. Most European gardeners would be horrified at the number and variety of large-scale pests that routinely harass American gardens. An enumeration of our natural enemies reads like a catalog of the kind of small private zoo kept by eccentric English nobility in the last century. You don't have to be way out in the country to participate in the struggle of man versus beast—most of these creatures have been greatly on the increase in the not-very-outlying suburbs in recent years, and now that they have successfully adapted, there is no reason to believe their numbers are going to decline in the near future. Not naturally, at any rate.

If you are like most ex-urbanites, you will probably enjoy having the wonders of the out-of-doors so near home. At first. That, after all, was why you bought this place. But after you begin to garden, and after experiencing a few episodes like the one I've just described, you may feel that the wilderness has come a little too close; after supporting an ungrateful menagerie for a while, you may be desperate for some kind of solution, if only for revenge.

LET'S SEE WHO'S OUT THERE

First, you should determine what pests you've got and what damage they're doing or are likely to do. (It is unfortunately true that occasionally people expend a great deal of energy exterminating some creature that is harmless, or even beneficial.) As with most problems, there are some pests we can live with and some that simply have to go.

Let's start with the worst: The villain of the opening scene was almost certainly a woodchuck. These large, dark-brown rodents, called groundhogs in some areas, are active mostly during the day from early summer to fall. They experience true hibernation, so whatever is eating your shrubs in winter is not a woodchuck. They are among the most infuriating of enemies because of the apparently wanton way they destroy plants. It often appears as if someone went by with a machete. Their taste is very broad and includes even poisonous plants like digitalis, wormwood and aconitum, which unfortunately appear to do them little harm. It is some solace to know that they have a high incidence of hepatitis remarkably like that in humans and many (30–40 percent) die as a result of liver cancer. But you probably don't want to wait that long.

As soon as you discover that you have woodchucks and begin talking to other gardeners about them, you will hear an astonishing catalog of solutions, many highly entertaining and ingenious but usually not very effective. A Havahart trap is often a first response. After driving around for several hours as you try to find a place to unload your furious passenger, you may decide you don't have a heart after all. Besides, a woodchuck den near your garden is like a subsidized apartment—there is always a waiting list. While you're out trying to dispose of your first catch, another is moving in. They have extensive underground dens with several active openings. Poison gas and smoke bombs work sometimes *if* you block all the exits and *if* the tenant is at home when you call. For a small area like a vegetable garden you can erect a low fence but you don't want to be fencing your entire property; besides, although woodchucks don't jump, they can dig extremely well, so although the fence can be short it must be set deeply into the ground so they can't go under it.

The next creature most likely to be on every gardener's blacklist is the rabbit. If you have woodchucks you may find it difficult to get as enraged at the rabbits—they are much more endearing creatures and wreak nowhere near the havoc caused by the competition. However, in the closer confines of the more built-up suburbs, they are serious plant consumers, and since they operate year round they can be counted on for girdling of trees and depredations of evergreen shrubs and smaller plants during the winter. They are also a scourge in the early spring, since all new shoots attract their attention. This is when they are the greatest pest; the woodchuck doesn't get active until later and tends to stay in the fields until the larger plants are up. Small temporary fences can be erected around bulb plantings until the plants are large enough to flower; needless to say this is a terrible nuisance, and unsightly. Nylon bird netting can be dropped over small patches of particular favorites until the flowers are fully developed. When plants are several inches tall they have less interest for browsers. Evergreen boughs used for winter protection also provide some deterrent; spread them on semievergreen plants like dianthus or hellebore even if their hardiness doesn't require it.

The last of the big three animal pests is the deer. These creatures, like rabbits, have the advantage of considerable personal grace and beauty—it may take several years to get really angry about the damage they do. You may have been outraged to find hunters roaming your land the first hunting season and promptly posted your boundary lines. After the demise of most of your young fruit trees and all decorative evergreens, you may not be so thrilled to drive in and find a deer on your front lawn. Ten years ago a deer ravaged your garden merely for a change of menu—increased competition for forage has now made dining out at your place essential. In rural areas with extensive woodlands and fields the deer is much more a pest in the winter when wild supplies are limited and travel difficult. They will eat all the young branches of a tree and strip the bark as well. Small evergreens (yews are a favorite) can be completely denuded. In more built-up areas they are active in gardens year round and will eat anything they can reach, though they prefer vegetables, bulb shoots and shrubs.

There are various chemicals that can be sprayed on plants to give them an unpalatable taste to deter animals. They will make herbs and vegetables equally unpalatable to humans and many of them leave a gray film that makes plants unsightly as well. Besides, as we discuss in detail later, the last thing you want to do on your weekend is spray noxious chemicals around the landscape. These sprays also can't be used in the winter because the sprayer will freeze. There are wire mesh or plastic tree guards available for wrapping trunks of young trees in winter—you can also cut black plastic into strips to protect the bark of smaller shrubs against mice and rabbits. Wrapping entire small evergreens in burlap is excellent winter protection.

The foregoing introduction to your animal neighbors mentions mostly non-solutions. One reason is that there are many more non-solutions than there are real answers to the problem. The other reason is that you have to be ready, psychologically, for the weapons that really work. Like most solutions they have their own set of problems. It is up to the gardener to decide which he can live with.

YOUR VERY OWN PREDATOR

One part of the overpopulation crisis of these animals is the decline in their natural enemies. One of the more "natural" ways of dealing with this is to support a predator of your own. Before you panic, I'm referring to a dog. (Or a cat.) It doesn't have to catch anything (though, given the chance, it will probably be delighted). It doesn't have to be large. It's true that your puppy's first charge through the border after a rabbit can convince you that you were better off with the bunny. But dogs can learn to behave in a garden as well as they can learn to behave in a living room. Some breeds have specific problems; terriers, for instance, have an irresistible urge to dig that is incompatible with the health of most plants. Any open expanse of dirt is an invitation to a dog to lie down and roll over. (Cats eye it with a darker purpose.) Females and altered male dogs are preferable in general because they tend to become territorial more easily and will patrol your property, not the entire neighborhood.

You don't want your dog to chase deer—this is neither necessary nor desirable (it's unlawful, for one thing). It is really only necessary for the deer to know a dog is in residence. There are many other gardens to choose from, and deer will always prefer travel to risk. Woodchucks and rabbits require more aggressive persuasion. The great virtue of a dog is that it will provide tireless vigilance, around the clock. Even if you are away all week, two days of energetic pursuit will make a difference that is immediately noticeable. Woodchucks, especially, eat close to their burrows. Weekend harassment is sufficient to keep them from setting up house close to your beds. Yes, there are many factors to consider before committing yourself to life with a dog, and a garden-

ing book is scarcely the place to go into detail about them (many readers may have decided I was crazy to venture this far with such a reckless proposal). The only argument I'm making here is that it really works.

MORE EXTREME MEASURES

The second recommendation may be even more foolhardy: Consider a shotgun. Not, let me hastily add, necessarily wielded by yourself—one of my husband's better shots blew a large hole in the middle of a hydrangea, and one of my early attempts beheaded an entire bed of sweet william. Neither shot did more than startle the woodchuck in question. (It should be said emphatically that all local ordinances should be consulted before you proceed.) You may be amazed to discover that some of your neighbors don't share your horror of guns and violence and might be delighted to come by and pick off a few woodchucks some afternoon when you're not around. Keep up your posted signs but begin selectively inviting responsible local sportsmen to hunt your deer. Ask for a venison kickback. As a longtime fan of Felix Salten I'm still a little shocked to be writing this, and I could never kill a deer myself (though I did get mad enough to kill a woodchuck with a shovel), but gardening in the country is bound to change your attitudes about many things; when you really get angry about the damage, you may be ready for the argument.

MORE PESTS TO PURSUE

After this slightly grim note, let's return to the zoo for a quick survey of other possible pests. Raccoons will do far more damage to your garbage and your vegetable garden than they will the other parts of your landscape, so they aren't a major problem—the dog will include them in its protection plan.

Skunks are a whole different question. They eat many harmful grubs and insects but if you have plants in small containers you may come out to find they have been tipped over and smashed as the skunk pursued the sow beetles that usually live underneath. Skunks are active at night, so if your dog or cat is out late, hope for the best. (In case of disaster, wash with tomato juice.) If you keep bees, skunks are much more of a major threat, since they will break into a hive and destroy it. In a case like that, or if one moves into your garage, poisoned scrambled eggs are often effective.

Even the city dweller can find squirrels becoming a nuisance—they will dig holes in any area of dirt they can find. In the suburbs they pockmark lawns and flower beds and harass bird feeders. Once again, the dog is your best friend.

Most gardeners greatly prefer cats to dogs—as you survey the damage done by moles, chipmunks and mice (in and out of the house) you can see why. Moles pursue all manner of soil insects and grubs, for which we are grateful, but in the process they heave up sections of lawn and tunnel under plants which then collapse from root damage. Mice use those tunnels to find bulbs, which they eat. There is a wonderful, medieval-looking mole trap that is sold, but it is extremely choosy about the kind of soil in which it will operate. (Besides, traps of any kind are effective only if you are around all the time to empty them. It's also remarkably easy to end up trapping yourself.) Your dog may decide that moles are on the hit list—mine did, when she ran out of woodchucks. The result of a ninety-five-pound dog in pursuit of a two-inch mole is breathtaking—I almost went out and got a cat. It is some consolation to those of us who try to garden in rocky clay soil that the moles usually can't be bothered to tunnel through that—they much prefer what is called "good garden soil." Some plants greatly resent root disturbance, but many return to normal if you water thoroughly when you notice that a tunnel has gone under a section of planting.

Chipmunks live in stone walls or in holes under trees at the edge of a wood. They'll bite the tips off any new growth—clematis seem a particular favorite—and devour the shoots of lilies as they come up. A cat is best, but chipmunks also can be poisoned with treated peanut butter inserted deep between the rocks. In the West the pocket gopher is a special nuisance. It shares many of the traits of both moles and chipmunks—it both tunnels and eats plants. It can be poisoned, but a cat is also effective.

Mice are mostly a winter pest. In summer they do odd things like bite all the seed heads off the poppies, but that isn't particularly irksome. In winter, however, they will lodge under some small woody or evergreen plant and chew every inch of bark from the stems. They will go through mole tunnels and eat bulbs (burying mothballs with the bulbs sometimes helps). They will move in under your winter mulch and set up house; when you take off the boughs in the spring you'll find that all you were protecting were several generations of mice—everything else is a stub. For this reason, cover up plants late, well after winter has truly set in and the ground is frozen. (This encourages them, presumably, to move back into your house instead.) A cat is the only real help, inside or out. If you are absent from the house for long periods in winter, poison is effective. Whenever you use poison of any kind, place it with extreme caution. If there is any chance that dogs or cats—yours or anyone else's—may eat poisoned animals, or if there are children of any age around the house or garden, don't use it.

If you have a pond, you may have muskrats. They usually confine their feasts to the plants growing in or near the water, but if you like water lilies, wild rice, willow trees or *Lobelia cardinalis,* you could suffer considerably from their presence. They can also weaken the structure of the pond with their burrows and cause it to leak. They are a difficult problem, since in the water they are faster than any dog and they are mostly nocturnal. Trapping within season is quite lucrative as well as effective if any of your neighbors is interested, but having had both a cat and dog caught in traps, I can't bring myself to recommend it.

I find it surprising that many gardeners set up numerous spinning, flashing devices around their gardens, presumably to scare off birds. A *few* kinds of birds are interested in a *few* kinds of seeds, almost all vegetables. Flower growers should welcome birds gladly, since they are nonstop consumers of insects and weed seeds. Cover cherries and berries with nylon bird netting (which is effective and practically invisible), and enjoy another dimension of your garden—hummingbirds amid the sparkling lychnis, a flock of goldfinches covering a thistle going to seed.

If I lived in an area where poisonous snakes were a problem, I probably would not have created the garden I have, which turns out to be snake heaven. The combination of a small pond with an acre of rock walls and terraces is irresistible to reptiles, luckily all harmless. Still, keep it in mind if you loathe serpents. I used to tell myself they were doing some good, but it turns out they mostly eat earthworms and frogs, both beneficial and preferable. In areas where poisonous species are prevalent and a problem, take all precautions, and consider the shotgun seriously.

If you garden in Texas, it could be an armadillo that is uprooting your plants at night. (What would an English gardener say to that?) The armadillo is in search of grubs, and is therefore on your side, but if it is doing much damage it's quite easily shot and is edible.

LIVE AND LET LIVE

At this point you are probably exhausted and depressed by this vision of a constant struggle against the wild (just wait until the next section, on insect pests and diseases). The most convenient way to discuss these possible gardening disasters is to lump them all into one chapter, but it certainly makes discouraging reading. Therefore, a note of solace seems needed at this point. You can always just ignore these animal invasions. Yes, it can be infuriating, but often the damage is not as great as it appears. Winter protection for young trees, shrubs and evergreens is most important and effective and can be done at a season of the year when there are few other demands on your time. Avoid plants like tulips that all browsers seek. Plant tempting broadleaf evergreens like rhododendron close to the house or the road, not way up in the woods, where you are making a present of them to the deer. You will learn slowly which plants are of no interest to the herds—use these at the far limits of your garden, like masses of naturalized daffodils at the edge of the wood. Utilize open, mowed areas like a no-man's-land—the closer the fields are to your garden, the easier it is for the woodchuck to slip in and out unnoticed.

Most of all, plant masses of plants and relax. Some will get eaten and you will be furious, but it's not the end of your garden. You may decide you prefer the deer to the rhododendron, the muskrats to the water lilies. This, after all, is what makes a garden your own.

THE INVISIBLE ENEMY

The foes we will take on next will make you nostalgic for the war of the woodchucks. One of the most infuriating things about insect pests is that much of the time the enemy is invisible. Something is out there, making holes in leaves, boring stems, warping flowers—and we never see it happening. Many insects are microscopic or highly camouflaged or nocturnal or so fast moving that it may take an entire season to figure out what is going on.

New gardens may flourish for a year, possibly two or three, before the insects partial to each flower discover that you are growing it. (The same holds true for diseases.) Then, the onslaught. You may find it fascinating to learn how specific insects are—many will eat only one family or sometimes even one genus of plant. On the other hand, you may be too furious to bother about natural history. All you really want to do is exterminate them all.

Country gardens suffer in particular from insect problems because nearby woods and fields are a constant source of new hordes. Don't feel that your garden is a particular target; a walk in the fields will reveal that a great number of flower stems there have those disgusting white blobs of froth on them, too, just like your plants. (In the center of the foam you will find a small insect appropriately called the spittle bug. Yes, it is eating your plant.)

Agricultural science has provided the gardener with a terrifying array of high-powered weapons for dealing with the insect world. If you are really prepared to go to war you *can* beat them, at least for a short time. But there are a number of serious considerations to be taken into account. I am assuming throughout this book that the reader has at least some interest in the basic ecology involved in a garden and in the larger surrounding environment. The environmental arguments against using broad-range chemical weapons are loud, convincing and are being made everywhere around us.

You have heard these arguments before; I can only hope you have some sympathy with them. But in many ways my other arguments may be more effective. I don't spray because I hate it. It is messy, tedious and enormously time-consuming. It can destroy marriages and sunder long-term friendships, since often the feeling persists that one *should* spray, and this generates the urge to make someone else do it. It is a perfect example of the kind of gardening chore that makes people hate gardening itself—it's difficult to keep in mind that it is the spraying you can't stand, not the garden.

Weekend gardeners especially have no time for hateful chores of limited effectiveness that threaten the environment. And these are perfect arguments to use, not necessarily with your neighbors but with yourself. When you see your hollyhocks turn brown with rust or watch the Japanese beetles devouring every flower of a cherished rose, it is hard to stand by feeling helpless when you think there is something you can do. Here are a few facts with which to reconcile yourself to inactivity.

To be effective, a spray program must be carried out regularly, usually every ten days to two weeks. You can't spray when it's raining. If it rains immediately after you spray, you might as well not have bothered.

You must know what your plague is to treat it properly. Not as easy as it sounds. It's very seldom you can see the villain in operation; if you do, will you know what it is? You can take a specimen for analysis to your local agricultural extension. This is the best method, but it is likely to involve not just *one* specimen but a dozen, of all the many afflicted plants you discover. Some problems are caused by insects, either on the plant or in the soil; some are fairly wide-ranging fungus growths, some diseases particular to one species of plant. Each will have a separate solution. Some may have no solution at all. Do you really want to get into this?

PLANT SELECTION FOR PREVENTION

Don't despair. There are many plants, far more than you will ever need to acquire, that have very few problems. There are other plants with a few out-standing problems that you can choose to ignore. Mildew is a good example of this type of problem. Lilacs get one form of this fungus; so do phlox, delphinium, roses, crape myrtle and a wide range of other plants. It is aggravated by climate conditions so it varies in severity year to year. For this reason too, it is much more a problem in humid areas with high rainfall. Free air circulation around plants helps. But much of the time it is a cosmetic problem that is annoying but seldom fatal. Some hybirds are resistant to mildew. But even plants afflicted with it can bloom and survive. (With roses there are so many other problems, mildew is almost a relief.) If your phlox look really terrible, cut them down. Yes, right to the base. They'll come back unharmed, and maybe next year it won't be so bad. Who really cares what lilacs look like in August? If some plant is completely overcome, pull it out.

This is part of the argument for a garden of lots of plants of lots of different kinds. You can always spare a few. If you have just one cherished specimen, you can be sure it will have some tragedy befall it. (This is also a way to deal with animal pests—it is unlikely they will eat *all* the plants you grow, or even all of one kind. If you can spare some tidbits in the front row the rest of the bed will usually pass unharmed.)

Insects and diseases, as I mentioned earlier, are often very specific. When you discover that the deck is really stacked against one species, give it up. This is part of my exhortation against prima donnas—don't put up with problem plants. You don't have time, it's unnecessary and it isn't worth it. Keep in mind that gardening is for fun. Also keep in mind why you want a certain plant. The apple, according to Bailey, has at least 400 major pests and diseases which afflict it. None of these need concern you if you simply enjoy your trees as a lovely flowering addition in the spring landscape. If you are seriously after fruit, you are committed to a spraying program from March to October. Wouldn't you rather enjoy your weekends and buy your apples at a local farm stand? And remember that the rose is a close relation of the apple and shares many of those afflictions. Although there are glorious roses that have relatively few pests, if the hybrid tea is the only rose that is a rose to you, get out the face mask and the malathion.

ALTERNATIVE WEAPONS FOR THE WAR

Even without spraying you are not completely without weapons. Some of them may be ecologically as suspect as spraying but are easier and more pleasant to use. I never said I was a purist.

Slugs and snails are disgusting and voracious—in some areas, like California and the Pacific Northwest, they are practically an epidemic, and affect seriously what can be planted. When the invasion is moderate, slug bait, usually some form of metaldehyde, is effective and easy to use. It also seems to be of little interest to birds, animals and other insects. If *you* are the purist, saucers of beer are the time-honored remedy. Dealing with just one pest (it's a mollusk, actually) may not seem like much of an advance, but slugs are common in all parts of our country, eat a wide variety of plants and flowers and operate over a long season. Getting them under control makes a noticeable difference for not much effort.

There are systemic granules available that are useful against *some* insects on *some* plants. The granules are spread around the base of the plant (as you would use a fertilizer, for instance) and dug and watered in. The insecticide is taken up throughout the vascular system; it kills insects that chew the leaves or suck the plant fluids. This method is used and extolled by many gardeners and it certainly is easy. Worth a try for certain specimen plants.

Ants are a problem because their digging disturbs plant roots and because the ants nurture aphids. The aphids attack your plants (in some parts of the United States there are ants that eat plants, too). Granules are available that can be spread on ant nests or around areas you wish them to avoid. These granules also deter or destroy certain other problem soil insects. They are easy to use and fairly specific. Ants can also be destroyed by pouring boiling water on their nests, but this is usually just a temporary measure.

Quite a lot of research is being done on the question of biological insect controls. This involves introducing a natural enemy or disease of a pest into your garden and hoping the best bug wins. This is a fascinating and tempting idea, but so far little has surfaced through commercial channels. One product along these lines which can be purchased is *Bacillus thuringiensis*. This disease attacks numerous harmful caterpillars. Another biological insecticide is the "milky disease" spore. This is spread on the lawn throughout the garden, wherever the grub stage of the Japanese beetle develops. Unfortunately, it is quite expensive, especially for use over a large area, and it takes several years before it is well enough established to affect the cycle of the beetle, but it is certainly worth the expense and the wait to deal with this problem in the long run. There are traps for adult Japanese beetles. These use synthetic hormones to lure the beetles to their death and they do work, but they also may lure greater numbers of beetles into your garden, where they will feed until they find their way into the trap.

Speaking of Japanese beetles—in July in some states gardeners speak of little else—one method is surprisingly effective and quite satisfying as well. You can pick them off by hand. This sounds impossibly tedious and time-consuming but against a small number of insects it works. It is also an excellent project for children—we protected my father's roses this way starting about age eight. Once you've got them, depending on your squeamishness, you can drop them into a jar of something or crush them with your fingers (as you get more and more bothered by these pests your squeamishness tends to diminish). This method works well against many of the caterpillars, too—there is a small green one that devours the leaves of aquilegia and can defoliate a whole plant in two or three days. The caterpillar works on the underside of the leaf and exactly resembles the edge of the leaf turning under. Two or three minutes of lightly stroking the leaves of the plant can rid it of the pests. Now this all may sound ridiculous, bending over a plant, scrutinizing the underside of a leaf; I find it fascinating, a perfect time to enjoy a flower up close, infinitely preferable to spraying, and it works, much the way swatting flies in a kitchen works. It seems impossible to make headway against the legions, but you can see improvement in a short while. Besides, each insect disposed of this way is a personal triumph.

Individual execution is also the best method against cutworms, large, thick, off-white or dirty brown grubs that chop off stems at the base of the plant. They live in the soil, usually right under the plants they're destroying, and are best dealt with by smashing with whatever weapon is at hand. There are products that are sprayed into the soil to eliminate almost all soil insects and grubs (they are also used against moles since they eliminate the moles' food supply). These are among the most dangerous chemical weapons on the market as they stay in the soil for several years and can easily enter the water system. Is it worth it for a few flower stems?

There are safer products that can be applied to plants to discourage insects. Rotenone and pyrethrum are natural plant derivatives available in dust form that don't necessarily kill insects but keep at least some of them off. Thorough instructions for the use of these products accompanies them when sold. However, if you are really nonchalant about this, the dust can simply be sprinkled over the plants with problems. It looks quite terrible on the plants, so do it Sunday evening—it will work all week while you're not looking. The simplicity of this is tempting and it does work in some cases. Often if you can protect a plant for three or four weeks, the crucial stage for the particular insect will pass and you can quit dusting, at least until the next plague shows up.

If you're fed up with insects we could turn to plant diseases. Or better still, if you have developed a horrible fascination for this topic, turn to a book like *Disease and Insects in Ornamental Plants* (Pirone, New York Botanical Garden), which enumerates practically all the garden plants anyone would grow and discusses every possible problem each one might have. Reading it makes me feel as I did when I took an abnormal-psychology course. Every symptom of every disorder starts to sound like your own, until your garden (or your psyche) appears a wretched mass of disease and decay, afflicted by every plague in the north temperate zone. It's not true, of course. You will never see a fraction of these problems. If you have large, valuable trees that appear to be afflicted with something serious, call a professional. These trees are irreplaceable and should be preserved at any cost; their care is likely to be beyond your capabilities.

MORE STRATEGIES FOR PREVENTION:
STARTING OFF HEALTHY

Avoiding disease is better than trying to cure it, just as health is better than good medical care. Buy only healthy plants—learn to look for misshapen limbs, leaves with strange marks or discolorations. Some of these could be the result of trauma but until you learn from experience how to tell the difference, avoid anything that could indicate illness. Learn from local nurseries and other gardeners what diseases are prevalent in your area. If you notice that all the wild plum trees have ugly black lumps along the stem, it's possible the cultivated plums could develop this fungus, too.

This may look like far too much effort for any weekender, but the terrace garden above is really less work than it first appears. One reason is that it doesn't rely on perfect maintenance for its effect. The edges are ragged and there are weeds everywhere, but the scene is still one of luxuriant and inviting loveliness. A strong overall structure of paths, steps and retaining walls guarantee year-round interest; the plant material is tough, easy and familiar, but used lavishly.

It's hard not to have a great garden in early spring, and the most effective approach to having one is usually the simplest. Bushels of narcissus (opposite) can be naturalized almost anywhere. They don't get eaten, they produce masses of flowers every year and you don't have to do anything to them. Very early bulbs like crocus are so welcome you can't have too many, and they can be spread in areas (below) that later become too shady for garden perennials. In this woodland setting their dying foliage will later be masked by an airy carpet of forget-me-nots. The sumptuous beauty of spring-flowering trees—a classic old apple, for example, shown at bottom—is another easy effect. The blooming time may be short, but it is unforgettable.

Dry-wall terraces transform steep, awkward backyard spaces into hanging gardens. Raised beds can be used to pamper species in need of perfect drainage and special attention, but they can also isolate invasive spreaders like the euphorbia and geranium at far left, used brilliantly together and kept away from the rest of the garden. Cerastium tomentosum (above left) turns a retaining wall into a sheet of white, highlighting the glowing red of the early Memorial Day peony. Bright blue perennial cornflowers (at the base of the wall) will pop up anywhere; their nice local name is "ragged sailors." A low wall (below) brings subtle detail closer to eye level: the delicate beauty of Nepeta mussinii and Gypsophila repens set off by stones.

Trees and shrubs, besides providing their own seasons of flowers, can shape your property and your planting. The gentle curve of the evergreen hedge at left makes a solid backdrop for a border and cuts off a view of a nearby road, while framing the barn in the distance. A naturalized shrub area (below left) forms a vivid contrast to the serene lawn dotted with trees. The shrub area makes an excellent transition to the wetland vista beyond. Paul's scarlet hawthorn, shown on this page, is a perfect small tree to use in a garden. In late spring, it has flowers like tiny clusters of roses. Foamy thalictrum and Endymion hispanicus *flower in the light shade beneath.*

Architectural elements also provide structure in your garden, and a fence is one of the most useful of these elements. The fence above makes the perfect backdrop for a narrow border; the precision of the picketing is a complement to the exactness of the planting. This is clearly the garden of a perfectionist. The picture above right is a good foil: Here the inviting curve of fence and path makes a garden out of an ordinary low-maintenance planting of shrubs and ground covers. Chairs (below) draw the viewer out to the edge of the woods, where a planted slope makes a delightful backdrop.

Don't overlook the area immediately around your house as a possible planting site—it doesn't have to be occupied by dull evergreens. Even mundane flowers (opposite) make an attractive foundation planting more in keeping with this simple structure than stiff shrubs. The planting below left contains nothing particularly wonderful but makes a colorful picture against the white background. The tall perennials are visible from the windows—from inside the house the planting has a totally different effect and makes a vivid foreground to the view beyond. The rich scent of the phlox comes in through the window in waves.

Vines provide unique flowering and foliage effects in your garden: They create graceful, sweeping lines and billows of blossom from arbors, trellises or fences, or add another layer of bloom to trees or shrubs. Wisteria (far left) hangs like grape clusters and spangles the grass below. Trumpet vine (above) can be a weed in the milder parts of this country, but with its attractive foliage and summer-long flowering, it's a weed with which most of us can live. Clematis (left) is often called the queen of vines, but that doesn't mean it's fussy. It can be grown in the coldest parts of America, yet it has flowers of almost tropical opulence.

A rose doesn't have to be a
hybrid tea rose. Week-
enders with little time or
patience should ignore that
demanding beauty and
consider instead some of the
versatile hardy climbers,
species and old-fashioned
shrub roses. A glance shows
how little maintenance the
climber at far right gets. The
garden has been abandoned
for years but the arbor bows
under the weight of the
flowers. The shrub rose seen
on page 143, Harison's
yellow, is shown above in
close-up. It blooms for
almost a month. Rosa
rubrifolia *(below) is a
striking bronze-leaved bush
over six feet tall, covered
with tiny single pink
blossoms in early summer.
Bright blue flax climbs the
wall in front.*

Many of the best known perennial flowers do best in sun, but shade is by no means a dead end. There are many hardy American woodland natives, like the dramatic cimicifuga (far left), that thrive in shade. In hot-summer areas of the United States, many traditional sun-loving flowers do better with at least some shade—the lily in the casual grouping below is an example. Callas (top) are not as tender as generally supposed and are ideal for dark, damp corners. In colder climates they can be grown as annuals for summer bloom; their sculptural beauty makes the effort worthwhile.

Ferns offer a variety of shady solutions; at far left, they make a graceful foundation planting. Ground covers don't have to be boring—sweet woodruff (near left) is a delicate, fine-textured mat sprinkled with tiny white flowers, used here as an underplanting with dramatic trillium and variegated lamium.

The versatile oleander (left) is so tough that it is easy to forget it's also beautiful. As a shady foundation planting around a porch, the oleander perfumes the sultry Southern air. Although hosta (above) is a universal shady cliché, here it is used with great flair, filling up the floor of a woodland with dancing patterns.

Alliums are ideal weekend garden plants. Hundreds of species offer flowers from the gigantic to the minute; most are undemanding about growing conditions and many are hardy anywhere. Allium christophii (above right) looks like a plant out of Star Wars. *It is unfortunate that A.* giganteum *(below right) is among the best known of these worthy bulbs, since it is not among the most reliable. Consider substituting more humble but accommodating leeks (above). If you decide you don't like them, you can always cook them.*

Don't be intimidated by the beauty of lilies; they're not nearly as hard to grow as they look. Although some, such as the lovely madonna lily (left), may be subject to disease, big stands like this are common in old cottage gardens. Grow them away from other species just to be safe. Too often lilies are grown only with other lilies, but you can see how effective they are in a mixed perennial group (below left), blooming here with thistlelike echinops and golden yarrow.

Elegant martagon lilies (above right) tolerate quite a bit of shade; because of the small size of the flowers and their subtle color range, martagons mix well in a woodland planting. Alstroemerias (above left) are called Peruvian lilies, although they're not true lilies and are mostly from Chile and Brazil. Superlative florist flowers, they are easier and hardier in the garden than generally thought and could be grown more widely in milder parts of our country.

Clump planting is a way to use large-scale flowering plants around your property without the complications of a perennial border. It may take nerve at first simply to plop down plants in the landscape, but certain features in your garden will invite this kind of accent, like the small pond below left. Magnificent Iris pseudacorus is completely carefree, given water and space, and the foliage stays handsome (and five feet tall) until winter. Day lilies (above left) are obvious candidates for clumps— here the clumps have spread and naturalized across an open field. Oenothera hookerii (below) demonstrates how just one plant can make a clump. This spectacular native western biennial is far too ebullient for a border. The big flowers of this evening primrose open at dusk; they unfurl so rapidly you can watch them like a time-lapse film.

More clumps for different settings: Peonies are often seen in old gardens as clump plantings. A majestic formal line (far left) marches away from a dignified home. The gas plant (near left) is another cottage garden favorite that benefits from lots of space. It is almost impossible to move, so the frequent upheavals of a border don't suit it.

You may not consider rhubarb an ornamental plant, but see (left) what a bold effect it creates in bloom. A clump of lythrum (above) dramatizes a water-side seat. Lythrum is so invasive only the foolhardy would let it near a border; on the other hand, who would want to pass up this blaze of purple in the doldrums of late summer?

It's hard to draw strict lines between clumps, naturalized plantings and meadow gardens, but they all offer lots of flowers for little effort. You can't, however, just walk over your lawn sprinkling wildflower seeds. The "meadow" below was sown on open, lightly cultivated ground. Quick-flowering annuals like these poppies and bachelor buttons can't compete in the long run with native grasses and perennial meadow flowers, but they sure make a lovely show the first year. The brilliant Shirley poppies add such grace to any garden that they should be allowed to self-sow freely in selected areas.

One of the best ways to learn what will grow in your area is to find old gardens and see what persists. This will also give you some idea of how to use certain plants. The sprawling phlox at far left, for example, should warn you of the dangers of using this plant in close quarters—here is an ideal clump plant. Lupines (below) have a reputation for being difficult, but if you see plants like these up the street, give them a try. The Oriental poppies in the farmyard at left tell you all you need to know— they're indestructible, invasive and gorgeous.

This cottage garden (far left) is a
nicely nonchalant mixture of garden
plants, such as dark purple salvia,
and local wild flowers like the pretty
pink musk mallow. Native weeds
and wild flowers are a great source
of garden variety but get to know
them before you let them loose in
your beds. Plants (left) that continue
to flower around deserted houses
clearly demand little upkeep. You
may not want golden glow for a
foundation planting, but you can see
it certainly isn't much work. Many
of these old-garden elements
(below)—phlox, ribbon grass, tiger
lilies, rudbeckia—combine in a
weekend cottage garden.

Two contrasting backyard scenes: Almost the entire area (left) of a rather confined backyard is taken up with a great sweep of flowers blooming in an energetic jumble. An ineradicable tree stump (below) becomes a featured planting site, breaking up the flat, open lawn. The stump has been surrounded with a planted dry wall offering vertical growing space to tiny campanulas and flowering thyme. Lavender and centranthus make larger masses of color and fragrance.

Rosa rugosa *is a tough and lovely shrub for difficult beach exposure; here* (above left) *you see it at the edge of a salt marsh. With its haphazard shape and vigorous spread, this is not a plant for a carefully groomed landscape. Let it loose on the limits of your land. Seaside weather and soil conditions usually guarantee hydrangeas of this astonishing color* (above right); *their long summer bloom makes them ideal beach plantings requiring little care.*

Most herb books seem to dwell on the need for a formal garden structure. As charming as a classic enclosed herb garden can be (left), such a garden may be too much effort at upkeep for a weekender. Herbs can be just as interesting— and beautiful—grown in haphazard masses (below).

Rock gardens are not all collections of tiny, unpronounceable and ungrowable plants sprinkled around boulders. In the garden above, an intrusive outcropping becomes a dramatic garden feature; the planting of cerastium and iris is stunning and utterly carefree. Rock plants (above, far left), even when out of bloom, have a fascinating range of textures that play against the rock surfaces. Aquilegia species (above, near left) self-sow and colonize any rocky surface in sun or shade. Blooming with them are armeria, verbena, saponaria and others. Natural stone steps (left) appear among a low haze of bloom.

After the lush June perennials have faded, the search begins for ways to keep color alive through the dog days. Rich red monarda (below, left), a striking American native with long summer bloom, contrasts with long spires of ligularia. Echinacea (above left), the purple cone flower, is a hardy beauty for the end of July, blooming here with salvia, coreopsis and cleome, a self-sowing annual. This is the time when easy annuals can add a lot—or even too much: Witness the Silene armeria *running amok (above). Bright blue is provided by Chinese delphinium, a self-sowing biennial.*

More midsummer combinations that succeed anywhere: yarrow and platycodon (far left); stokesia and coreopsis (near left); two variations on color contrasts. All these hold up well in hot parts of our country. Centaurea macrocephala and eryngium (below) may sound threatening, but they grow easily and make a stunning textural display.

Is this a meadow (left) or a meadow planting? If you can't tell, it's a success, and a great way to bring flowers to a low-maintenance part of your property. The tall purple thistles may be a little too natural for everyone's comfort.

Sequence of bloom is one of the obsessions of perennial gardeners; don't let it drive you crazy when you're just getting started. It's not necessary to have every part of your garden flowering all the time. On the other hand, there are natural, easy combinations that can ensure an area doesn't go dead after two weeks of bloom. The scene below is the late summer version of the picture on page 147. Self-sowing opium poppy, dill and clary sage take over from May perennials; dramatic ribbon grass comes forward late in the season. All will look great until hard frost.

Here (above right) is a spring combination, a detail of page 147; below, the late summer succession tritonias that aren't supposed to be hardy come back anyway to bloom with Queen Anne's lace.

Those of us with early frosts console ourselves with the glories of autumn foliage and the spectral effects of senescence and sudden death. In milder climates, lovely Japanese anemones bloom from September until late frost (above, far left). The tree hydrangea (above, near left) is a star of the close of the season and provides material for winter bouquets. The silvery artemisias (below) linger to the very end, here in the company of the native New England aster.

The Japanese call it borrowed scenery—using the garden to frame the landscape that surrounds it. Gardens don't have to be enclosed. One of the glories of a country garden is the magnificent scenery that often accompanies it. If you've got it, make the most of it.

Good garden hygiene can make a big difference. Cut off any diseased leaves or stems at once and dispose of them in the trash or in the fire, *not* in the compost pile. Healthy, robust plants are less susceptible to disease and recover quickly from insect injury. Good air circulation reduces the incidence of fungus diseases—you can plant thick clumps out in the open, but leave more space between plants in stagnant corners. Don't leave piles of weeds and clippings around the beds or on the lawn or paths—this material decays rapidly and attracts insects and slugs (mice will also hide or nest there). Be ruthless with diseased plants and get rid of them quickly.

Your choice of plant material is what matters most in coping with all these problems. We know delphiniums aren't easy for a variety of reasons. I may have convinced you that roses are a bad bet. You will discover a few more limitations to what you can grow, and experience a few setbacks in your gardening career. That's infinitely preferable to spending your weekends hauling around a five-gallon backpack sprayer and filling the air with what could turn out to be the next decade's DDT. You will be able to nibble a stalk of parsley or spearmint without having to race into the house to scrub it first. Watch your children tumble in the grass without wondering what residues may still be lurking. In learning to avoid or ignore insect and disease problems, you can still have a garden full of flowers and have more time in which to enjoy it.

6

INEVITABLE UPKEEP

No matter when spring arrives in your garden—depending on your location on this vast continent, it could be anytime from February to May—it is a time of exhilarating and frantic garden activity. Here are all these seeds you ordered back in the depths of winter. Did you really send for sixty rosebushes? And what about those enormous clumps a neighbor dug out and generously gave to you? You haven't even taken up your winter protection yet and the planting projects are piling up in the cold frame by the back door. Two days a week is nowhere near enough time; you are barely inside the house except for occasional quick meals, and you return to real life on Monday with aching bones and dirty fingernails you may never get clean. For a few years you may believe that this will never happen again, that *this* year you will really get things under control and in the future spend spring in leisurely appreciation of your garden. But it doesn't happen that way, and it shouldn't. After months of restless and rainy inactivity, it is a real joy to be out of doors again. (Primitive peoples celebrated with bonfires and rites of passage—you may find a pleasant echo of this as you haul off the winter mulch and burn it).

All the frantic overload of work matters least now—the impetus of the season carries it along somehow. New plants and new projects generate their own enthusiasm. What I really set out to write about in this chapter is the work that, for most people, has no enthusiasm to carry it along. We can call it basic upkeep, what is needed throughout the season year in, year out to keep the garden from going back to the wild or worse. Some call it maintenance—most call it drudgery.

WEEDING: DELIGHT OR DRUDGERY

This is the job which exemplifies for most people, especially nongardeners, endless, futile and boring garden activity. I suspect these people began life weeding vegetable gardens. There are few more depressing sights than a long row of almost microscopic squash plants engulfed by purslane, quack grass, burdock and sow thistle. It astonishes me that anyone grows vegetables. However quickly the peas grow, the weeds are quicker and infinitely more vigorous. And your brief triumph at having liberated one section is tempered by the fact that a row of potatoes, however well grown, is just not that beautiful.

There are a lot of definitions of a weed—every garden writer has a favorite, many of them coy or silly, like "a flower out of place," or "a plant that is misunderstood." A weed is a plant you hate—that, I think, is a good start. After that, a weed is a plant you don't want; that one is important, too, because after your garden becomes established, you will find that many of your greatest weeds are plants you planted in the beginning.

One of the first things to begin learning—and continue to learn as long as you garden—is the weed population of your area. For a few years, you may as well be resigned to burdocks you mistook for digitalis until the subtle differences become clear. Perhaps you assume that you know what you planted, and everything else must be a weed. Well . . . each new seed packet adds to the unknown, as do pots bringing two or more invaders along with the original purchase. Then there are confusions you can never straighten out: In our area there is a very pretty and horribly invasive bellflower which resembles several cultivated campanula species widely offered for sale. You never know which one is in your garden until it has settled in forever. Some nurseries even sell— and garden books extol—plants like aegopodium, bishop's weed, which cannot be eradicated by anything less than continuous application of a powerful weed killer.

I should make my position on weeding clear before we proceed: I love weeding. It is one of my favorite parts of gardening. It is solitary, contemplative, completely absorbing and not terribly hard work. Had I world enough and time this is how I would spend my day and my garden would be weed-free—need-less to say, it will never happen. And I know most readers don't feel that way, though that might be the fault of the vegetable garden. If you are turning to flowers from vegetables, you are in for a wonderful surprise. It's not that flowers don't "get" weeds. But perennial plants fight back—their large size and enor-mous vigor give them an easy edge over most annual weeds. And weeding perennials, rock plants or herbs is both interesting and pleasant. This is a chance to see your plants up close—see how the buds are forming, spot a few self-sown seedlings coming up in an unexpected place, enjoy the rich aroma of the rose-mary, notice how one favorite is completely taking over a corner. Don't think of it as a chore—much of this is pleasure. Develop your own strategies for mak-ing it exciting: For instance, notice how easily dandelions come up just before they flower. Try tracking down a snakelike bindweed root to its origins. Work after a rain or thorough watering when the ground is soft and yielding. I usually weed parts of the garden that are just coming into bloom, because that's when people are going to be looking at them; also, it's a nice time to be around the plants. Weeding can be one of the first chores of the early spring and the last of the fall—when it's still too soon to work the soil after winter and you're dying to get out and do something, it's an excellent time to go after those grasses that settle inextricably at the base of some plants. Every area has its worst weeds and every gardener has particular foes he's sworn to conquer. My worst enemy is grass; in a garden as tangled as mine almost anything could pass for an intended plant, but everyone can spot grass and know I haven't been keeping up.

WEEDING OR MULCHING: YOUR CHOICE

There are a few shortcuts in weeding. Chief among these is the use of various mulches, which are also important (as we will discuss shortly) in preserving moisture in the soil and reducing watering. The chief difficulty in the use of mulches is the look of them. In some situations, like the vegetable garden, if you don't care what it looks like, black plastic is a powerful ally. Besides retaining moisture and smothering virtually all weeds, it warms the soil and helps ripen tomatoes and peppers and other vegetables that grow slowly in a cool summer. But there's no denying that it is unsightly in the extreme, and it works best where plants are grown in straight rows. It can also be used under stones, brick or gravel when a path is laid. It will eventually disintegrate but it can give a few years weed-free head start before plants start to sprout. Stone paths and paving are among the hardest areas to keep weed-free, too, since roots wedge deeply between the stones.

In areas of greater visibility—around shrubs or young trees near the house, or among newly planted clumps of plants that will eventually grow into a large mass—one of the loose, large-chunk mulches like pine bark is appropriate. Many towns have trucks that chop up fallen trees, branches and leaves into a mixture perfect for this purpose—some places will even deliver a truckload if you ask for it. This is worth looking into, since this kind of mulch is less uniform and more natural-looking than a commercial product and is also (usually) free. It has the advantage, too, of being appropriate to your locale—this is important to consider, since it affects the way it will look in your setting. In some regions salt hay is widely used—this is excellent for winter protection, which we'll discuss later, but looks messy in general use. In the South, pine needles are an attractive favorite. You need something that can be spread deep—several inches—but still be unnoticed. Avoid at all cost the familiar "garden-center special" look: a few juniper and rhododendron dotted in a sea of pine-bark chips.

Flower beds call for something even more unobtrusive, something that can be spread easily among the plants, that stays neat and remains effective and doesn't distract from the flowers. I'm not sure this exists. Cocoa bean shells, peanut husks, coffee grounds, sugarcane, grass clippings, peat moss—all of these have adherents and all have drawbacks. Peat moss can be a useful soil conditioner and many people love to spread it on a bed because it looks like very clean dirt; it is a disaster as a mulch since when it becomes dry it hardens to an impenetrable imitation of plywood. Peat moss and pine needles will also eventually make the soil acidic, so lime should be added to balance this. Some of the others will provide soil nutrients when dug into the bed, but may rob it of nitrogen in the process of decay. Several of the above have their own peculiar odor you may not want competing with your flowers (the idea of gardening amid coffee grounds is particularly disgusting).

A chopped-leaf mulch is lovely material to work with and few things are better for the soil. When handled discreetly it can work to reduce weeding and watering. If you have access to a shredder you can make your own in the fall. Apply a thick layer late in the season—after the ground freezes—for winter protection. In spring move the mulch away from the base of your plants as they come up—mulch close up to the stems encourages insects and fungus growth. Keep an eye out for mice nesting here too. As it starts to decay and be less effective as a mulch, dig it into the soil and add a new layer.

Weeding or mulching, you'll soon discover your own preference; the style of your garden, too, will determine how you use either or both. One kind of solution is heavy mulching of shrubs and newly planted trees and mulching of large-scale plant clusters seen at a distance (these will have little need of mulch after they are established). Beds of more choice perennials should be hand weeded. Once the bed gets going and the plants fill out, they really won't need much attention either, as the season goes on. Herb gardens can go either way— the perennial herbs are so vigorous they are almost weeds themselves; annuals from seed may need more help. If you are set on a formal structure for the herb garden, mulch would not look out of place. In the rock garden a gravel mulch is used but it doesn't really deter weeds—most love it. The gravel mulch provides a fast-draining surface that keeps soil dry on top, cool underneath— almost all plants thrive with this situation, weeds included.

CONSTANT VIGILANCE—THE PRICE OF WEED CONTROL

You are never going to be able to keep weeds from entering your garden but cut down on their opportunities whenever possible. In a country garden, the closer the fields come to your flowers, the more field you will have in your beds. Design your garden so a wide swath of mowed area stands between you and the rest of the plant world. Many seeds will still be wind borne into the garden but you can eliminate quite a few this way. Supposedly the heat of composting kills weed seeds but some always seem to persist; try to keep bad perennial pests out of the compost pile and dispose of them separately. Look carefully in manure for root sections of invaders like bindweed or quack grass and eliminate them. Eye container-grown plants with suspicion—they may be carrying new weeds you could do without.

If you are plagued with something really ineradicable, like aegopodium or equisetum (horsetail rush), you may have to resort to a systemic weed killer. This is a fairly desperate measure and must be done with extreme care. Although it is a tedious business, painting the weeds with a brush is often preferable to spraying and risking the rest of your plants if the wind shifts. This is an argument for trying to keep the worst weeds out from the beginning if pos-

sible. If you have new topsoil brought in, cover it completely for a few weeks with black plastic after it is spread, before you plant it. This will kill the weed seeds in the top few inches (just remember not to turn the soil deeply when you are ready to plant).

It's worthwhile having a separate seedling bed, since these tiny plants need greatest protection from weeds. Here you can prepare the soil with extra care, mulch heavily and sow seeds in rigid rows. Besides getting new plants off to a

Lack of space is no excuse—in fact, what better way to make a nondescript house into a country cottage than by filling every inch with flowers? Here there is no question of closing out the neighbors or framing beautiful views; don't worry about that intimidating term "landscape design." Just take the land you've got and make it alive with color and fragrance. A planting like this makes a home personal, individual and inviting.

good start, this gives you a chance to get to know new species you may never have seen and may fail to recognize in the weedy wilderness of the rest of the garden.

One strong vote in favor of hand weeding is that it is necessary for successful self-sowing, one of the principal methods for filling your garden with plants and keeping tricky annuals and biennials coming back each year. It's not going to work if you mulch properly, since your mulch is indiscriminately smothering all unexpected seedlings, weeds and flowers alike. This is where knowledgeable weeding is most rewarding. Only you (we hope) will spot the choice seedlings and let them be—at least until you find that purslane is no longer a problem but your garden is overrun with Shirley poppies or *Silene armeria.* Besides creating a garden, you then have the satisfaction of knowing that the weeds you grow are your own.

STAKING UP OR STAKING OUT

Why do plants fall over? This must be one of the most infuriating things to have happen—just when some big, gorgeous specimen is about to flower, it comes toppling over in a crash of broken stems, squashing the delicate, smaller plants in front of it. They usually do this during the week, when you're not looking, so you're greeted with chaos on Friday night and spend Saturday morning trying to unscramble the mess. Often you can learn from your plants and the way they fall what the problem is. Some flowers, usually super hybrids, have been selected to produce the most enormous flowers possible. The blooms are way out of scale with the plant and the stems simply can't hold them up. Sometimes, in your effort to provide all the best things in life, your plants are overfed—stems are enormous and quick-growing and not very strong. Sometimes toppling over indicates that a plant is ready to be divided—the stems splay out in a wide circle from the center. Plants reaching out toward the sun will often go over in an attempt to reach it—all will fall in the same direction. A big plant with shallow roots on sandy soil will often go down like a tree in a storm, with the entire root system exposed. This can also happen from mole tunneling. And some plants, even small ones, always fall over, however they are grown.

There are also large numbers of plants that will stand like soldiers under any conditions. These are on the top of our planting list, obviously, and you may be surprised by the number of tall, impressive plants that need no help.

The majestic *Fritillaria imperialis* rises unaided above the entire garden in early spring. None of the numerous allium, even *giganteum,* ever needs a prop. It always seems impossible that the huge wands of eremurus sway gently throughout their long season without snapping, but they do. I am amazed every year that my hollyhocks don't fall over—there are some advantages to heavy soil and poor cultivation. Yucca and verbascum provide highlights in midsummer, erect even at six feet. Likewise liatris and lythrum, all those spikes and masses of purple in July and August; you would need a backhoe to tip over a lythrum.

Some big plants like Oriental poppies may flop but they always keep their heads up—if you grow them in separate clumps away from anything else, it won't really matter—just cut them back after they flower. This should be done with any plants that sprawl after blooming—cut back ruthlessly before they smother something else. Peonies always fall—those enormous heads just pull the stems to the ground. Even if you surround them with little fences, as some gardeners do, they flop over the top of them. The answer here is to cut lots of peonies and let the rest go. Cut the heads off when they look terrible, and the foliage usually straightens up by midsummer. As with poppies, they should be growing separately. The lovely single varieties, besides being exquisite, usually stay upright.

There are plants that always spread around awkwardly in a bed; some of these are best used planted in a wall. Veronica or *Campanula carpatica* will flow down the rocks in a sheet of sparkling blue; *Cerastium tomentosum* and arabis make waves of white. Try growing inveterate sprawlers like baby's breath on top of a retaining wall, so they sweep down in a mass of froth. Gypsophila is actually one of the easier plants to stake—disregard books and catalogs that show how to truss it up in a straitjacket. Because it is so light, just a few twiggy sticks stuck up under the mass will keep it off the ground. Often, if it is growing among stiffer plants (try it with echinops, for instance) it will hold itself up on their stems.

Most of your garden can be made up of plants that either don't require staking or ones that can fall with grace. But there are always a few tall, irresistible beauties that you decide you must have. Then you have to figure out how to do it so the plant and not the stake is the focal point of the garden.

One recommended staking procedure, especially for lilies, calls for placing stakes in early spring, just as the plant comes out of the ground. As you can imagine, this results in a garden of sticks waiting for something to happen. The most unobtrusive stakes can be made from natural sticks—long suckers cut during pruning are excellent. If they are slightly twiggy on top, so much the better. These can be stuck in the ground around the plant after it is well along in growth but before it starts to flower. You want to provide support but keep a graceful, natural shape to the plant. Tie in several places up the length of the stem. This is all a fairly tedious business and takes some practice at first—a good argument for short plants. Some gardeners develop a real knack for it, though, and can stake everything in sight without anyone's seeing a stick.

If you are in an area of frequent and violent thunderstorms, or if you have a problem with wind, a sheltered location is important for growing taller plants; even with a windbreak, you may find staking essential. In sandy soils, too, it may be the only way to grow certain plants successfully. If you have a whole line of tall plants—across the back of a bed, for instance—that topples forward, a mass approach could be effective. Run a line of nylon bird netting—stoutly secured at each end—across the middle of the bed in front of the topplers. They will lean gently forward against the net, which will be shielded from view by the shorter plants. This works best if there is a hedge or a wall at the back of the bed; that will protect the bed from wind and keep the back row from heading over the other way.

Some leggy late-bloomers like Michaelmas daisies can be handled in another fashion. Cut back some of the plants—the ones in front—in midseason to about half their height. This won't stop them from blooming—almost nothing can stop this plant—but they won't reach their full height and the cut plants will flower later than the tall ones, which you'll probably have to stake.

Staking is like most garden chores—how much you do depends on how much you can stand and on whether or not you get to it. You can have a lovely garden with no staking and lots of plants leaning on one another or tumbling about—you may notice some of this in the photographs. On the other hand, if you have a mildly compulsive nature you may even enjoy staking—your eight-foot-tall delphiniums will be the envy of us all.

WATERING: WHETHER YOU MUST, WHETHER YOU CAN

What if it doesn't rain? This is a question of concern to anyone who cultivates the land, from the weekend enthusiast to the giants of agribusiness. In some parts of this country, there is generally sufficient rainfall throughout the gardening season—if there isn't, gardeners have always assumed they could water. Several years of intermittent widespread drought and more stringent watering restrictions have (I hope) sharpened our awareness of the need to conserve. A few gardening practices can aid this conservation and save the gardener's time as well.

Proper soil preparation is a major conservation measure, besides being necessary for any aspect of good gardening. Soil with lots of organic material will both retain water and drain well—this is not a contradiction. The organic matter holds water particles in even distribution around the roots of the plants and allows for sufficient air circulation, letting the soil "breathe." Heavy clay soil, by contrast, either sheds water or holds it in stagnant pools which drown the roots. Sandy soil permits the water to pass through too quickly, taking soil nutrients with it.

It's not always necessary to water when you see plants droop—some do it at the first sign of heat, regardless of water in the soil. Shallow-rooted plants like phlox go limp at little provocation. Usually it takes no more than a cool evening to revive them. They do best if they receive some protection from the hot sun in the afternoon.

When you must water (and if you *can* water), give plants a long, thorough soak. This works well with a weekend gardener's schedule, since one thorough watering (about one inch of water a week) is all most plants need. This is a good time to mention one of my favorite garden gadgets, the rain gauge. I'm sure there are elaborate, expensive forms of this available but the best is a small, clear plastic box sold in local hardware stores for about $3.50. It's a truly worthwhile investment. Even if it's not *necessary* to know to the tenth of an inch how much rain you've had in a week, you may find it more and more fascinating— it will become one more thing to scramble out to see with the flashlight on Friday night.

Keep in mind that plants under trees can often get drier quicker than the rest of the garden. This is because once the soil gets dry, it takes more rain to penetrate the leaf mass overhead to wet the ground again. Also, tree roots compete with the smaller plants for moisture—this is true of plantings close to shrubs, too. Don't assume because it *looks* cool and damp under there that it necessarily is.

In large areas of this country, gardeners can count on no rain whatsoever for long stretches. We discuss this in more detail in the regional sections but I want to mention the problem here because the key to gardening in this kind of climate is plant selection, and gardeners in other parts of the country have much to learn from this. There are large numbers of native plants that not only survive hot spells or drought, they need them to flourish. It means that much of the garden goes dormant in midsummer, but this is also a time when most gardeners would prefer to do the same. There has been increasing interest in growing more of our beautiful wild flowers—many of them, certainly, are not easy, but if you have this kind of climate, nothing else is going to be, either.

Mediterranean plants often do well in the face of high summer heat and no water—they are, for the most part, a flexible group of plants that thrive in a wide climate range. These are most familiar to us from the culinary herbs—one reason the herb garden looks fresh and undeterred throughout hot, dry periods. There are many relatives of these plants that aren't for eating but make lovely, often scented, often silvery shrubs and ground-covering mats if the winters aren't severe and the summers are.

Rock-garden plants are another group well suited to summer drought. That bare expanse of rock and gravel may look unbearably hot to you but, in fact, it's the opposite. Each stone collects water under its surface and protects it from evaporation—the rock surface gets hot but reflects heat from the soil underneath. Also, most high alpine plants in their natural setting experience great extremes of temperature change; constant wind aids evaporation of scant rainfall. All these factors have resulted in plants with little stem and leaf surface and long, thick roots ideal for reaching deep moisture and storing it.

In the rock garden a gravel mulch effectively conserves moisture—it can do the same in other parts of the garden, but it usually looks terrible. This is less true along a rocky coastline or in western areas adjacent to desert—there, with a careful use of local crushed rock or gravel, you can create an overall landscape where this kind of surface is visually effective and useful. But in lushly growing rural areas, bright gravel scattered around trees and shrubs just looks like the driveway is escaping.

A mulch of chopped bark or leaves will keep the soil from drying out too quickly. When you water, try to direct the flow *under* the mulch—you want the water to sink in, not just splash around the surface, and the mulch will actually work better if it's kept dry on top. Sprinklers are better suited to watering a lawn than a flower bed—most plants are better off without water splashed on their leaves. Soaking hoses work well, especially if you can soak deeply around the plants and leave the open spaces between them dry—there's no point in watering a new crop of weeds.

When you move a plant, water it in thoroughly, cut back the top, then mulch heavily with anything available, regardless of what it looks like—it's only for a short period, and water retention is essential while the plant is getting reestablished. Seedling plants, with their barely developed root systems near the surface, need greater protection than anything else—another argument for a separate seedling bed of highly water-retentive soil. Keep this well mulched and shaded from too-strong sunlight.

In general, plants should be grouped according to water needs—flowers of a damp woodland simply won't survive with alpines or Mediterranean shrubs that flourish on rock. Plants or bulbs requiring summer dormancy should be apart from perennials requiring some watering in midseason. In this way you can reduce the overall area that demands watering in dry periods.

What about automatic watering systems? My personal feeling runs strongly against them. They are one way in which our landscape can be depersonalized, divorced from both the climate of the surrounding area and from the demands of individual species of plants. They can prevent a gardener from really knowing the needs of his garden. Automatic watering systems are best suited to a prefabricated yard with little diversity—the familiar lawn-shrub-specimen-tree layout, for instance—or for a very specialized planting with specific needs, like a formal rose bed. In near-desert climates, an automatic system is practically standard equipment. You can use it creatively to ensure the health of important trees and shrubs, but don't make it a weapon to defy the natural landscape of your area.

However, automatic watering can be helpful to weekenders in one place: the propagation bed. Seedlings and newly divided plants, as we noted above, have greater water needs than established plants, and if you can't water at all during the week, in dry periods these susceptible plants may suffer, although light shade and heavy mulch can make a big difference in survival. If you confine your efforts at propagation to a small, separate bed, a very limited timed watering arrangement could be set up. (This is also the place to keep new arrivals you haven't had time to plant in other parts of the garden.) I myself am extremely wary of anything involving plumbing or timing devices—I prefer to pay a dependable neighbor to come in once a week for twenty minutes. Or I let the plants take their chances.

You can learn a lot about your garden in a period of severe drought. Most of us feel as if we ought to water when we can. When you can't water, you may discover how little really was necessary. Well-established perennial plants generally need far less water than annuals because their root systems are large and go deep into the soil. A lawn will look terrible before anything else, but except in severe cases it will usually survive, particularly if it is made up of varieties native to an area. If you find you must struggle constantly to keep it—and in many parts of the United States this is true—consider turning it over to a rugged ground cover, native or otherwise: mesembrayanthemum, various kinds of sedum, crown vetch, wild thyme—these are only a few possibilities. They are not everyone's idea of a lawn, but in a drought, your ideas may change, often for the better.

CUTTING BACK

Cutting back, pinching back, dead-heading, pruning—these are practices endlessly extolled by all basic gardening texts. Some gardeners seem to make something of a fetish of it, nipping off every growing shoot, often, it seems, even before it flowers. (I have, in fact, seen one rock gardener on hands and knees with nail scissors, trimming off each tiny leaf as it yellowed.) We're told that if we keep at it, our gardens will be immaculate and our plants will bloom continuously. As with many gardening myths, there is some truth in this, but in one sense it doesn't matter how true it is—we will never be able to practice it assiduously enough to know.

Annual flowers try to complete their cycle of growth in one season; if they are not allowed to produce seed, they go on producing more flowers until they can. But climate and weather play a part in this, too; some cool-weather flowers like lobelia, verbena, calendula or alyssum keep going until it gets hot; at that point all the cutting in the world can't encourage a yellowing, sickly looking plant. Anyone who has grown peas or spinach has seen this happen, too—at some point, the plants have simply had enough.

Perennials respond in different ways to cutting back. With some, you can produce a second, later flush of flowers. With others you won't get another bloom, but cutting back is necessary to keep a sprawling, leggy plant from flopping all over the bed. Most of the bulb plants produce only one flowering stalk per bulb, whether you cut it or not—you are urged by most books to cut off the spent flowers to keep them from going to seed, but most of the hybrids aren't going to produce seed and I have always found it made little difference to the strength of the bulb. This is the kind of cosmetic dead-heading a weekend gardener can easily skip until there's time, or forget about.

Most traditional gardening books have a horror of plants going to seed— perhaps, for these writers, self-sowing represents the first step toward chaos, the garden taking off on its own; this must be guarded against at any cost. Clearly this is not the kind of gardening we're talking about in this book. The weekend country garden has at its heart an enjoyment of the interplay of cultivation and chaos, natural order and disordered nature. Self-sowing can lead to messy gardening, but it also produces an effect of exuberance and grace utterly absent in a highly groomed border.

Some plants produce seed pods as interesting as flowers—if the plant stays attractive, leave them, enjoy them and pick them in the fall if you are a dried-flower enthusiast. Baptisia, with its fat, rattling pods of blue-black, and dictamnus, with spikes of star-shaped capsules and spring-loaded seeds, are good examples. I would go mad removing spent heads of Siberian and Japanese iris; they must number easily over a thousand and I'd never get to it even if they weren't decorative—luckily, they are.

It's not easy to know at first which plants must be cut back, which will bloom again, which you will want to self-sow and which you can forget about. A lot, obviously, depends on your sensitivity to untidiness. (Don't forget, too, about those plants you can't cut back at any cost: Bulb foliage must be left until it withers.) One pleasant way to experiment is to pick lots of flowers. The weekend gardener has little need of a cutting garden. If you are away all week or not spending time in the garden, pick big bouquets to enjoy until next Friday. Take them to the office; give them to friends who have vegetables. Some of the plants you are growing will probably not make good cut flowers but this is how you find out. On many flower stalks you can see places farther down the stem that will sprout when the top is cut back. With some, whole new shoots will emerge from the base of the plant—you won't know until you pick the first crop.

Pick or dead-head annuals heavily when they first start to bloom—the flowers are usually nicest then. Later in the season, or when the plant appears to be giving out, let some seeds ripen and fall, then pull out the whole plant.

Many early-flowering perennials are so messy by midseason that even a really sloppy gardener gets fed up and chops them down. When you find they continue to flourish, you'll realize cutting back is not something to be timid about. Oriental poppies, *Cerastium tomentosum,* perennial cornflowers, *Veronica* "Crater Lake"—all these are best handled with a lawn mower as soon as they've flowered.

Pinching back is a fairly specialized technique quite different from cutting back. This refers to the practice of removing the growing tip of a stem early in the season, both to promote thicker, bushier side growth and to delay flowering. It's an important procedure for seedling annuals which might otherwise race into leggy, premature flowering; perennials, too, can benefit from it the first year since it aids good root development. It's hard to bring yourself to do it—most of us are so thrilled to see seeds growing we can't bear to deliver a setback—but it's beneficial in the long run.

Some even more fanatical specialists pinch off the side buds on shoots of plants like "football" chrysanthemums and dahlias. In this case they're aiming for one super-enormous flower. It works, if that's what you're after; I can't imagine that many weekenders have either the interest or the time.

Let your own limitations of time and space and your tolerance level for disorder set the limits of your cutting back. It's an important and useful technique and, when you have the time, a pleasant one to practice, wandering through the garden with a basket and clippers. Just don't feel chained to the secateurs and don't forget all those chance seedlings you might be giving up. They are the flowers that will make your garden most alive.

Pruning is really just another variation on cutting back, although the term is usually used in connection with woody plants. This is one gardening "chore," unlike weeding or staking, that has many enthusiasts and it's easy to see why. For one thing, much of it is done in the late winter or early spring; it's a great time to be outside (for limited periods of time) but far too early to do any serious gardening. Pruning of young trees encourages compact, sturdy growth in the shape you want—it's hard, at first, to part with any growth made by a new favorite but almost immediately it's apparent how a tree thrives with this treatment. Pruning old apples is even more exciting—from an overgrown shapeless mass slowly emerges the gnarled and beautiful outline of an ancient tree. Fruit trees like this become a particularly appropriate form of sculpture around your property. There are numerous pruning handbooks to tell you the fine points of the art but you can figure out most of it for yourself, especially since you're not intent on producing a fruit-bearing tree. Once you've liberated your tree from suckers and dead and diseased branches, feel free to follow any eccentric outline this particular specimen may offer.

Your shrubs may need to be pruned periodically and this is a source of some confusion—do they bloom on new wood or old; do you prune in midsummer or early spring? (If you grow shrub or species roses or hardy vines the same questions arise.) Most woody shrubs bloom on branches formed the previous summer—if you cut back hard in early spring you will lose the flowers for that year. The easiest way to keep track is to cut back after flowering, but in the busy periods of spring or early summer you may not get around to it. One pleasant way to deal with it is to cut the branches just *before* they flower, and enjoy the bloom indoors, during the week. With early spring flowerers— forsythia and quince are the obvious favorites—you can prune very early and force the branches practically in midwinter. Don't worry too much about an ideal timetable—most plants are not that tricky. If you are really worried about when and how, it's usually better not to prune at all. Most flowering shrubs with sufficient space to spread can do well without a yearly trim. Remove dead branches periodically when you get a chance—this can be done at any time. It's most important to let your schedule of leisure time dictate your pruning—or any other garden activity for that matter. What usually happens is that suddenly at the height of summer, your place seems like a jungle—get out the loppers and establish some order; your shrubs will bounce back with renewed vigor next year.

HOW MUCH TIME IS ALL THIS TAKING?

Let's stop a moment to take stock of these chores and just how much time you may expect to spend on them. I usually practice basic maintenance in a pattern that could be called "crisis intervention." After the spring onslaught, the garden often goes along without attention for several weeks (as I write this book, for instance) until some event triggers the need for a few hours of concentrated effort. I then storm through a section, weeding, cutting off, propping up or just pulling out things that don't look good. One mixed border six by twenty-five feet (after literally no care for over a month) was in great shape in just under an hour; another, more complicated planting eight by twenty feet took one and a half hours. This is not a recommended gardening practice, but it is the way most of us work. These are well-established plantings; any new or newly replanted areas will need more time at first. I bring this up to show that really very little time is involved in most of these chores—we may find some of them tiresome but they're not particularly time-consuming. Chores like staking arise sporadically throughout the season and, unless you are a fanatic, require a little effort here and there, not a big block of time. Pruning is usually done when there's not much competing for your attention. When the weather turns dry in midsummer you may have to water, but you'll be weeding less. In the cooler weather of fall everything slows down and you'll have time to move things around and plant more bulbs.

Special care should be taken to keep clear paths, steps and paved or gravel areas. It looks charming at first when self-sown foxgloves show up to soften the effect of a new path, but you'll soon realize that many plants prefer to grow wedged between stones. Suddenly you're seeing more flowers in your brickwork than in your beds. It's also really hard to get them out. Try to be ruthless about this: Not only is it inconvenient to be jumping over plants as you walk along, but it destroys the visual, spatial structure you are trying to create. Your beds can be in wild chaos if your paths preserve a sense of order; these are the bones of the garden and must be allowed to show; keeping mowed areas in good order has much the same effect.

You may find that certain parts of your garden seem to need attention much more often than others. If you find you are always fiddling over something in one area, try to figure out the problem. If the soil in a bed was not properly prepared, weeding is more difficult—you never get the roots out, and the plants don't grow vigorously enough to keep ahead. Perhaps a particularly invasive weed has gotten control. Perhaps these are just not the right plants for this location. It's worth the time to redig the bed or change the planting rather than fuss over it every week in this annoying fashion; once a good perennial planting is established, this kind of constant work shouldn't be necessary.

LAWN CARE: THE LESS THE BETTER

Perhaps I should say a few words about lawns here, since I've failed to mention them so far. A well-kept lawn can do a great deal to set off advantageously a house and garden—this is an obvious fact realized by everyone from eighteenth-century designers of the great English landscapes to cut-rate developers of suburbia today. Attitudes toward lawn care range from the fanatical—the frantic homeowner out plucking dandelions and crabgrass—to the lackadaisical—me. I'm definitely in the school of if-it's-green-it's-a-lawn; luckily I live in a part of the country where I can get away with it, since all I ever do is get it mowed. *Not* mow it myself, please note. One of the greatest time-saving strategies for any weekender is to get someone else to mow the lawn. Mowing the lawn is an essential part of creating and maintaining order in your garden, but once you determine how and where it should be cut, buy an excellent mowing machine and find someone to use it. This is one of the few routine garden chores for which it is possible to find someone—your time and energy are better spent elsewhere.

If you have a good climate for grass, lawn care will consist of almost nothing besides mowing. (Agricultural science has finally caught up with laziness and now recommends that grass clippings be left unraked to feed the lawn.) If you don't have a good grass climate, and find you are spending most of your gardening time fussing over your lawn, try to consider alternatives. In some settings, even if you *can* grow grass, it's much easier not to and it could be more appropriate to your landscape to take another approach.

SOIL UPKEEP: WHAT COULD BE MORE BASIC?

Soil upkeep has few enthusiasts. In a book it tends to be dull for writer and reader alike, which is why many books skip it; in practice it's plain hard work. But there's no getting around the fact that it is probably the most essential part of overall garden maintenance. After a few years of rampant growth, your original row of tiny perennials has become a bed of enormous plants. What they're feeding on to support all this growth is the soil, and sooner or later that food supply starts to give out.

Inorganic, commercially available fertilizers, either in granules or timed-release globules, can help in the short run. In the spring and intermittently throughout the season, these are spread on the soil at the base of the plants and lightly scratched in. It's also a good practice whenever you're moving a plant or are transplanting seedlings to add some soluble fertilizer to the soil in the hole before you place the plant. If used too heavily, or if these materials come into direct contact with parts of the plant, they can cause some damage; used properly, they can be a helpful tool in feeding your plants, but there's still a long way to go toward solving the overall problem.

The first chapter of this book discusses necessary soil preparation and emphasizes the importance of organic material. What we have to do after initial bed preparation is to find a way to maintain the organic content of the garden. In areas of thin, porous or sandy soils with persistent short bursts of rainfall throughout the season, organic material disintegrates very quickly and nutrients are leached through the soil with depressing rapidity—this is a common situation in the southern states. Seaside gardens have much the same problem. Heavy clay takes untold quantities of organic matter before you can even begin planting it—after that, new clay often works upward when the frost heaves it.

Mulches used for drought and weed control will slowly disintegrate and can be dug in. In the fall, leaf mold, compost or aged manure can be spread between the plants and worked in further in the spring. It may seem as if the soil is higher than the plants in places—it may be for a while but frost action, snow and winter rain will help it settle in and gradually molder into the rest of the bed.

This process gets harder as your plants get larger and closer together. Periodically it's best if you take everything out and start over; although it's harder work than spreading fertilizer or compost, it's much more satisfying. This involves digging up all resident plants in an area, setting them aside, and redoing the bed almost as if you are starting from scratch. In your earlier attempts at garden making, you may not have prepared your beds quite as well as you should have; even if you did, it's amazing how many rocks work their way up in a few years. This is also a great opportunity for ridding yourself of some of the more persistent perennial weeds that have plagued you. You're probably ready to rearrange some of those early planting combinations and try out something new. Ideally, you should do this late in the fall; stick the old plants in a holding bed and leave the bed empty while the soil settles and all the new organic matter rots away into perfect condition for the spring. If you can't get to it in the fall, or if you want to replant right away, just be sure to use more mature manure, or very well-rotted compost.

DIVIDING AND MULTIPLYING

All this ties in well with our next topic, dividing your plants and expanding your garden. You may be happy with your first little bed, but after a few years your plants will be huge and looking for new worlds to conquer. Some plants demonstrate their readiness for division by making enormous clumps but few and puny flowers; some get spindly and lank and fall over. You can put off the inevitable for several years with some plants (and there are plants you can never move or divide), but sooner or later you've got to dig most of them up and start a whole new garden.

The recommended times for this are spring and fall, but depending on your weather and rainfall patterns, you can do it whenever you have the time. One general rule is: Move spring bloomers in the fall, fall bloomers in the spring. This is so you don't miss a season's bloom, but if your plant badly needs dividing you're not missing much, and if you are redoing a whole bed it's much easier to take everything out at once. In cool northern regions with adequate rainfall, August is a fine time for this work since there are few competing garden chores and the garden tends to be at a low ebb; major excavations in the spring are fairly intrusive. In other areas, fall is a season of drought but late winter is mild and rainy and therefore propitious.

Most books on perennials tell you how often they must be divided, but don't feel this is an invariable timetable. Different climates and growing conditions will affect this aspect of a plant's growth as well as all others, and the necessity of dividing will vary a lot, even in different parts of your garden. Many books seem to discourage gardeners from growing perennials that need this attention often but if you are an eager beginner with a country garden to fill up, you will probably be happy to be propagating new plants so easily and rapidly. Now, where are all these new plants going to go? Perhaps you've discovered belatedly that one species is bent on taking over the entire bed—this is probably a good candidate for making a big clump off away from more highly controlled areas. Once you find you have this wealth of plants—and have gained some confidence about growing them—you may be more prepared to let some species take their chances at the limits of your garden. Keep closer areas for delicate, slow-growing or slightly fussy plants and let the giants fight it out with the wilderness. A new bed or one newly replanted will require a little more attention than your established plantings. More watering may be necessary, depending on the time of year, and mulching is a good idea here to prevent drying out and to control weed growth. Newly turned soil, manure and compost produce a whole new crop of weeds you'll have to eradicate—the recently divided plants will need some time before they fill the new space. There's a temptation to fill up this space with annuals but don't try it from seed—buy plants or transplant from other beds; starting seedlings will confuse both your weeding and your mulching.

One of the joys of making a garden is giving it away. You may have been pleasantly surprised at the eagerness with which gardening friends passed on great mounds of plants when you first started out—now you understand why. You, too, will be looking for new enthusiasts to encourage when you begin to see the overload multiplication by division can provide.

If you are not redigging a whole new bed you can, of course, lift a plant, divide it and set one portion of the original back where it was—take this opportunity to enlarge the hole and dig in lots of compost or manure. The size of the divisions depends on the arrangement of the root system in some plants—you may see several major roots tangled around one another and after unscrambling the knots, there are your new plants. The more common arrangement is a large solid mass with many roots of more or less equal size—just slice the whole clump in half, or into thirds or as small as you like ("just slice" usually means with an ax or a pick—don't be nervous). You may prefer to pry pieces apart with two garden forks. Smaller portions may give you a few more years before you must divide again, but you'll have quite a gap to fill up in your bed. Often it seems, too, that larger portions settle back in more easily. If you want to try out the plant in another location, a bigger plant gives a sense of the desired effect at once.

PLANTS ON THE MOVE

Which brings us to the question of moving plants. The answer is yes. Never be afraid to move a plant. There are exceptions: Deep tap-rooted perennials like *Asclepias tuberosa*, baptisia, dictamnus are moved only at your peril; some members of the Umbelliferae—parsley, nigella, Queen Anne's lace—don't transplant well; most of the poppies, both annual and perennial, resent disturbance. All books on perennials make the point emphatically about these few— it's unlikely you'll have a major tragedy. But most gardeners err on the side of overcaution in this respect, and that is not only unnecessary, it's bad for your garden. The best books by real gardeners—Gertrude Jekyll, Margery Fish, Vita Sackville-West, Elizabeth Lawrence—are full of plants being hauled up and around, tried out in new places, yanked out and moved again. The plants really don't seem to suffer—in fact, sometimes it takes several moves before you find the special site in which a species thrives.

Occasionally, when it is said about a plant that it is difficult to move, the meaning of this is somewhat other than what you expect. It could just mean that the plant is likely to die, but in the case of the Oriental poppy, this is not exactly the problem. For years I hesitated to transplant them because of such a warning; finally I got fed up, dug up the enormous roots and moved them. They looked ghastly, appeared to expire, then came back with a flourish. So did the ones in the original location. I have now been zealously digging out the same poppies for years—huge snakes of root appear, are discarded (only to take hold in the compost pile); still, every spring, the poppies turn up undeterred.

If the plant is simply being moved around in your garden, not being divided, it usually doesn't suffer much of a setback. If it is late in the season and the top of the plant is huge, cut it back hard to reduce water loss and strain on the roots. If it is in full bloom you may hate to do this, but use the blossoms as cut flowers.

Newly moved plants need slightly more attention just after the move, especially in midseason when the weather is hot. The plant should be watered thoroughly and mulched to retain moisture. A light screening from bright sunlight is a help—if you are around for a few days after replanting, put a big carton over the plant in the heat of the day, then uncover it at night. Even two or three days of this attention will produce a transplant that looks as if it had lived in its new spot forever.

Don't go on being dissatisfied with a plant in the wrong place—seize the trowel. You'll spend less time moving it than you did in worrying about whether you should. This is another step toward greater freedom in your gardening style; when you realize how accommodating most flowers are, you can be more daring in your planting schemes. A few fatalities should not discourage you. You'll even find that some plants do better when they're always on the move.

AUTUMN

Once the hard frosts become more insistent and the garden really begins to wane, you may start facing the possibility of autumn cleanup. If you have been zealously cutting back, this probably isn't much of a problem, but I suspect most weekenders just kind of let things go at the end of the summer. I know I do. So the beds and clumps are very likely now filled with senescent plant material and the whole landscape may look pretty disheveled. It's quite satisfying to go around and cut everything down to a tidy basal lump. This also makes it easier to spread winter protection over the plants. On the other hand, it's often very helpful to have old shoots sticking up from plants like platycodon or asclepias— new growth appears so late in spring that I frequently hit them with a shovel during early cultivation unless I have a skeleton there to warn me. Last year's growth is also a good reminder of just how big some of these perennials can get—we all forget over the winter. In some cases the old stalks and leaves help to protect the plant from winterkill and discourage early spring browsers. In short, you can feel good about autumn cleanup either way, whether you do it or not. Don't you wish you had more chores like that?

WINTER

When I think of gardening in California, or in any climate without a winter, I remember an Irish acquaintance being told that the bars in New York are open all night. This Dubliner turned to my husband in awe and said, "Well, I don't know how you stand the pace!" You don't, of course, *have* to garden year round (or drink all night), but there is something nice about having a very definite end to the gardening season. We in the North might wish winter were a little shorter or a little less definite, but I am quite ready to see the garden go when it must and be happy with the thought that I can do it all over next year.

But this is not a time of total inactivity. A few preparations should be made to ensure that the garden comes back more or less intact. Providing winter protection is not a difficult or unpleasant job and it can make an enormous difference in how much garden you'll have next April. There is usually not a great deal competing for your time now either, besides a few football games on television, and most of these projects can be done a little at a time.

You may be absent from your country house for a long period in midwinter but you can be sure that the deer are still around. Any evergreen, broadleaf or coniferous, is a possible meal. The smaller shrubs are best wrapped completely in burlap. If you have rhododendron planted in clumps, a burlap "fence"—open at top—can be made around all at once. Slender, upright shrubs can be wrapped up to five or six feet—the deer won't usually go higher than that. Deciduous shrubs that carry large and tempting buds through the winter—magnolias, for instance—can be covered with bird netting. The bark of young trees may be gnawed by deer or rabbits—there are plastic or wire guards for the trunk that are helpful. Often smaller shrubs will be chewed by mice—tree guards are too big for these stems, but you can make your own with strips of plastic bags.

Evergeen foundation plantings may be safe from deer but are in danger of falling snow and ice from the roof—these can smash the center of the shrubs. Many people make simple, permanent A-frame shelters for them from two hinged boards. (Some people may simply decide to dispense with evergreen foundation plantings.)

Deer don't usually become too bold until after hunting season, and rabbits and mice become bark eaters only when all other supplies have diminished, so you can install these protective measures late November through January depending on your schedule and regional climate and snowfall—it's much more difficult doing all this when there's lots of snow on the ground.

Cold is a much more substantial adversary than a herd of deer but your best protection is what you've been practicing all along—proper plant selection. Besides the effect of the cold itself, the combined action of freezing and thawing that occurs in early spring is what usually takes the greatest toll on perennial plants. Some are literally thrust up out of the ground by this movement. A heavy mulch offers protection by keeping the ground frozen until temperatures are more uniform and the ground can thaw slowly. It can be left on more sensitive plants to protect tender growth from late frosts. It also offers new bulb shoots some protection from rabbits.

The best winter mulch—and the easiest to obtain—is evergreen branches. Dry leaves of the nonmatting variety (like oak) are also good but you have to have something on top of them so they don't blow away. You can put evergreen branches on top of them, or you can forget the leaves and just use the branches. This mulch is best applied after the ground is solidly frozen, which means the best time is right after Christmas, when everyone except us gardeners is discarding the Christmas tree. Fir and pine are preferable because they hold their needles and aren't as prickly as spruce. Get out the loppers and spread the resulting pieces over the beds. Some plants and some beds need more protection than the rest, but you may not remember which is which once all the plants are dormant—just cover everything with a thick layer. It occasionally happens that snow arrives before your mulch—don't panic. Snow is the best possible natural mulch; if we had snow cover all winter we wouldn't have to worry about all this. Besides, the weather you're protecting against occurs in the spring. If you want to be out in the snow, spread your branches roughly where you think your beds are; you can place them more exactly when it melts. In treeless coastal regions, salt hay is often available and is a useful winter mulch. Ordinary feed hay is equally effective but has the distinct drawback of distributing seeds of every possible local weed and grass throughout your garden.

Don't be too eager to take off your mulch—do it gradually, uncovering first very hardy and early-blooming areas like the rock garden. If your area has sporadic late frosts, take even more time before clearing—the new growth will proceed more slowly at first but catches up quickly. It's worth the wait if you can save your lilies from that one last freeze. Even after spring is in full flower, I keep some branches handy to throw on at night in an emergency. When you are finally in the clear (you hope) don't add this mulch to the compost; brittle woody branches like this keep softer material from settling in to rot. Celebrate the new season with a mulch bonfire (if local laws permit) and get ready to get back to gardening.

7

A FEW
SPECIFIC GARDENS

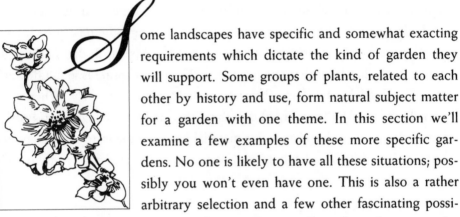 ome landscapes have specific and somewhat exacting requirements which dictate the kind of garden they will support. Some groups of plants, related to each other by history and use, form natural subject matter for a garden with one theme. In this section we'll examine a few examples of these more specific gardens. No one is likely to have all these situations; possibly you won't even have one. This is also a rather arbitrary selection and a few other fascinating possibilities had to be ignored for lack of space. You may learn from these examples how unified plantings develop in response to natural conditions; through this you may see possibilities for your own landscape and garden.

THE HERB GARDEN

August would be reason enough to have an herb garden. When the rest of the landscape is looking pretty worn out, herbs have a freshness and vigor that remains undeterred by heat, drought or disease; many of them are just coming into bloom. The culinary herbs are at their peak now, perfect to accompany the quantities of fresh vegetables your neighbors are giving away. Growing these plants, using them, drying them all give such pleasure that it is easy to understand why man has cultivated herbs for thousands of years.

Besides all that, herbs are wonderfully simple to grow. This is the perfect garden for the real beginner, particularly a timid one (it was my first gardening attempt fifteen years ago); it is hard to go seriously wrong with these plants. Most come easily from seed, even the perennials—this is a good start in growing perennial plants, because even if they don't flower the first year, you can still use and enjoy their savor—you don't feel you have to wait two years for something to happen. (One note of warning—real tarragon cannot be raised from seed. The species for which seed is available, so-called Siberian tarragon, has virtually no flavor. Start your tarragon by buying a few plants, then dividing them.)

Herb gardening has greatly increased in general popularity in the last twenty years (you are no longer considered a witch if your garden contains henbane or aconitum); as a result, there are many retail sources for seeds and plants, both for the most familiar and the really out-of-the-way. Part of this interest is related to general trends in cooking—the use of herbs is now widespread in most of the popular cuisines available in America (fresh-cut herbs can even be found in surprising variety in supermarkets throughout the country), but this culinary interest scarcely explains the sudden trend toward growing woad or costmary. People are growing them again, I think, for the reasons people have always grown them—they are fascinating plants. They are not all beautiful plants, and in this way they are a wonderful lesson for the gardener just starting out. It is through plants like these that we realize that much of the greatest pleasure in gardening does not come from simply producing enormous and beautiful flowers. Herbs, with their subtle textures, peculiar and fascinating aromas and odd habits of growth, encourage greater sensitivity to the entire range of the plant world. These are plants with both character and history—there's something irresistible in growing the plant that turned the Britons blue two thousand years ago.

Another reason an herb garden is a good garden for beginners is that these plants, however odd their individual appearances or habits, grow well together and present a coherent visual impact. This is an enormous help to someone trying to work out a planting scheme for the first time.

Many of the traditional herbs were originally Mediterranean plants—be prepared to experiment to see which do best in your climate. In the North, marjoram is a tender annual and must be started early indoors—in mild climates it makes a perennial mat or small shrub. Coriander and summer savory are fast-germinating and fast-growing annuals which quickly provide more plants than you can use, no matter how short your summer. Chervil grows and flowers so quickly you can have two crops a season—it performs best in the cool weather of spring or fall. Basil, on the other hand, responds best to heat and sun, like the tomatoes it accompanies so well—in my short, cool summer both are hopeless. Perennial plants that die back up North take on a completely different character when they can grow year round—the sages, for example, become large and striking shrubs instead of low mounds.

Most herbs have similar simple horticultural requirements: Full sun and good drainage are the imperatives; most prefer lime in the soil, and most do best if the soil is not terribly rich. There are always exceptions, of course, and there are bound to be a few plants that are fussy in your particular climate or soil, but given the above conditions, you can grow all the basic herbs and a lot of eccentric additions as well.

Many gardeners prefer a formal layout for their herb gardens. I think this may be because the plants themselves are so vigorous, weedy and unruly that they seem to require a rigorous structure to keep them under control. Attractive though these formal gardens are, there are few things that require more maintenance than a knot garden or a parterre; these are out of the question for a weekend gardener, and turn a part of the garden that is virtually maintenance-free into a gardening obsession.

The annual culinary herbs are best grown separately in small beds; these can be arranged in a somewhat formal manner if you wish. Have these near the house, if possible, so you can run out easily (usually in the dark) to pick them for supper. Thyme, marjoram and curly parsley make good edgings; lavender, southernwood, hyssop, santolina and upright germander provide small hedges. It's fun to grow a big bed of silvery-leaved plants together—there are a great number of them available and in late summer into the fall they make a refreshing sparkling mass in the hot sun, ghostly and brilliant later under moonlight.

It's nice to have your herb garden separate in some way from the rest of your plants; as a collection they will have more of an impact. It's also important to try to keep some of these plants contained as much as possible—some of them even need protection from each other. All the mints are extremely invasive, and chives, catnip, tansy or yarrow will soon empty a bed of any other occupants. Some herbs, while not invasive, just get very big—baptisia is quite slow-growing but eventually makes a mass like a shrub; rosemary, in climates where it's hardy, does the same.

The range of herbs for your garden is enormous—it really depends on how strict a definition you wish to employ. Once you start looking through the considerable library available on this topic, and running through a few retail catalogs, you'll realize that there are many more possibilities than you have time or space for. Start with the basics—herbs for cooking, both annual and perennial—and some of the most familiar edgings and hedges to give a structure. A few large shrublike perennials can provide focal points—baptisia, dictamnus, one large peony. *Rosa gallica officinalis,* the apothecary's rose, is appropriate, and the other ancient European rose species complement it. Junipers make perfect evergreen accents; in mild climates rosemary and bay also flourish year round.

In the herb garden much of our attention is on the plant—the fragrance and texture of the leaves, the stem structure and habit—but don't overlook all the possible flowers. Calendula, opium poppy and nicotiana are three of my annual favorites for late summer—these will self-sow in most climates. Allium and salvia are two enormous genera which contain numerous traditional herbs for cooking or fragrance; I include many of the less well-known species from each because they have interesting or lovely flowers and look right in my garden's setting. This is one of the ways you can stretch your own definition of an herb garden to include the plants you want to grow. So many garden flowers have been used in either medicine or cooking through the ages that it's easy to find justification for almost anything you like. Sooner or later you will find an authority who includes a plant you want to grow. Be guided by the overall look of a plant—remember that this is no place for the flashy hybrid or the exotic.

Most of the small, very early spring bulbs can't really be considered herbs by any definition but the herb garden is an excellent place to grow them. The beds for annual cooking herbs will be empty until late spring—by that time species tulips, *Iris reticulata* and early crocus will be long gone and even the foliage will be ripe for removal. A well-drained site near the house is fine for these first glimpses of spring. Since most herbs don't get started early this will add another season of interest to this part of your garden.

Do I use all my herbs? Well, in all honesty, of the more than seventy herbs I grow, I regularly use about a dozen. I suspect that many more serious herb growers than myself, when closely questioned, might admit the same. I have herb books and I even know what all these crazy plants are for, but when it comes to making absinthe from wormwood or dyeing my new wool (what new wool?) with baptisia, I just never seem to get around to it. I can't imagine substituting a leaf of borage, which has a texture like used steel wool, for an inoffensive cucumber in my salad; it self-sows every year, has flowers of an amazing, vibrant blue and keeps the bees happy, so I don't feel it owes me anything. Someday someone may show up here with a really persuasive recipe for hyssop omelets and I'll be ready; until then, I'll enjoy its pungent, skunklike odor and charming flowers and use it the way I use all my odd herbs: for the pleasure of growing them.

It's not just the rather exacting horticultural conditions that contribute to the look of the seaside garden. There is the dramatic contrast between the powerful natural scenery and the often frail, often frivolous, often temporary structures man has constructed at its edges. Somewhere between these conflicting forces you want to make a garden, and it's going to be a challenge.

The biggest and gaudiest of the annuals seem more at home in this setting than in any other—Monet's painting "The Terrace at the Seaside, Sainte-Adresse" has always seemed to me to convey the quintessential beach-resort garden. Geraniums, petunias, annual salvia, lobelia and alyssum all flourish and appear more brilliant, partly because of moderate temperatures, cool evenings, high humidity and full sunlight, partly because of the severe backdrop offered by sea oats, cedar shingles and sand. There's also something gay and temporary in the whole atmosphere that makes these plants look appropriate. Since many houses or cottages in this kind of location are rented, often for short periods of time, these plantings seem to be the only kind that make sense, but if you own your home (or rent every year for a long season), don't feel that this is the limit to what you can grow.

If your weekend house is not right on the beach, your gardening problems are pretty much the same as everyone else's except that your climate will be somewhat better and your soil will probably be quite a bit worse. Many shore gardeners fear salt spray as their greatest enemy—this will depend a great deal on location and prevailing winds but it's seldom as serious a problem as most homeowners expect, once you are even a few hundred yards away from the beach. In an occasional hurricane your plants may suffer from a strong blast of salt but it's likely at that point that you'll have other things to worry about.

Soil is a more definite problem. Water races quickly through coarse sand, leaching out any available nutrients and draining too fast to help parched plants on the surface. Sparsely growing trees and shrubs add little natural organic matter. Sandy soil *does* have two great virtues—it's easy to dig and it supports few weeds. But in order to grow anything, quantities of organic material must be added, and they must be replenished frequently. Coastal soil is usually at the acid end of the scale, with a good supply of available iron—one look at the triumphantly blue hydrangeas, blooming in this setting like nowhere else, will show you that. Lime-loving plants are best grown in separate beds to which limestone can be easily added. Soluble inorganic fertilizers can be a help—apply frequently in small quantities throughout the season if you are growing plants that prefer rich diets.

Let's create a hypothetical garden that *is* right on the water, since this is a favorite fantasy of many of us, and some of you may even be living it out. In one way the limitations on the variety of usable plant material will work in your favor here: Beach plants are a self-defined set which survive in this harsh environment because of a few modifications which they share. This gives them a similar appearance, even if the families are unrelated, and this similarity is a great help in working out a harmonious landscape if you remain sensitive to your surroundings and the natural flora. Site analysis is of great importance here. If your cottage is huddled among sweeping dunes, stay with those long, low lines. Constant wind and sandy soil are a combination that eliminates tall, bulky plants. This is a landscape for low mounds and mats, with occasional sturdy accents.

Perhaps your area of coastline is the dramatic, rock-littered vertical variety. Clearly much less planting will be necessary here, or even possible, but many of the same plants which do well on the dunes will be at home, once they become established in crevices and ledges. The mats and mounds just become cascades up and down the rock face.

Sand dunes support a very delicate ecosystem and in some places this unique life has come, of necessity, under the protection of the law. Find out, before you start, if there are limits of that kind on your property. Even if there are not, respect native vegetation: Learn from it and use it whenever possible for the framework of your garden. See how the habits of local plants suit your site and let that be a guide. Even these native seaside plants may suffer damage occasionally—new growth in the spring can be injured by heavy salt fog; high tide levels and hurricane winds in the fall often take their toll—but native plants are able to recover from these setbacks more easily than inland species.

Beach plum and bayberry are two East Coast natives that could be planted more on either coast. They make irregular-looking shrubs and some gardeners might consider them untidy, but they thrive in the poor soil of seaside settings and they have their own specific character. The beach plum blooms very early—delicate white flowers tight along the twiggy dark stems, like every Chinese painting of spring; too early if your beach days start in June, but welcome to year-round weekenders. Bayberry, the original source of the candles, has glossy dark semievergreen foliage; the "berries" are small, hard, dusty gray, in stemless clusters surrounding the lower part of the stem. The entire plant is richly fragrant. Both these plants can be difficult to grow away from their natural habitat but are carefree within it. Consider them for eccentric accents.

Rosa rugosa is not native to either of our coasts but it has naturalized so successfully that most of us assume it has always been here. The handsome, shiny, wrinkled foliage stays attractive for a long season and the shrub produces flowers continuously until fall. There are double hybrids and many varieties of color available but the classic rugosa flower is single, deep pink or white, with a bold shock of gold stamens and a heavenly fragrance; if this isn't enough to sell you, the hips are as large as cherry tomatoes, bright orange and full of vitamin C. The bushes frequently carry flowers and fruit at the same time. It's a big bush and irregular in shape—too rough and wild for small gardens, perhaps, but a great windbreak or informal hedge in larger layouts.

Another candidate for our category of ungainly but interesting native shrubs is baccharis. Barely visible flowers are followed in late fall by seeds with a fluffy white pappas—the entire shrub looks like a silvery mass of froth in October and November. It thrives in either sandy soil or brackish swamp.

The two most commonly seen hardy olive trees are likely additions for your seaside landscape. *Elaeagnus angustifolia* and *E. commutata* make large

Learn to work with the challenging landscape and growing conditions of your seaside property. Stick to ground-hugging mounds of salt-tolerant species with minimal soil requirements. Taller accents and windbreaks can be provided by native coastal species like baccharis or bayberry.

shrubs or small trees of graceful outline. The flowers are not conspicuous but richly scented; the fruits, which persist on the tree long after the leaves fall, have an amazing opalescent surface. Both species are extremely hardy and carefree—they can be seen naturalized in many coastal regions and are frequently used as plantings along highways, a tribute to their toughness.

I envy waterfront gardeners their tamarisks; this lacy tree/shrub seems to revel in a heavy diet of salt. (Keep this lovely plant in mind for the salt-laden soil of western desert regions, too.) Settled in sand just above the high-tide mark, it persists under impossible growing conditions; the delicate twigs, like branches of bright green coral, produce a haze of pink foamy blossom in summer.

Although the horizontal junipers are an overworked landscape cliché in the suburbs, in the bare and windswept coastal regions they can provide a perfect background for herbaceous plants and offer year-round interest in the landscape with virtually no maintenance. There is a bewildering assortment of hybrids and cultivars for every climate, however extreme; just take care, when making your selection, not to end up with a "juniper sampler"—one each of twenty varieties. Use large masses of one or two kinds for ground covers, another type for edgings, perhaps, then one or two upright forms for accents. You want to create a landscape, not a collection of horticultural oddities.

Many silvery-leaved plants, even ones not originally native to the seaside, do well in difficult beachfront locations. The silvery effect is caused by a covering of hair on the leaf—this offers protection from desiccating winds and bright sunlight. These plants look right with the native vegetation and provide an excellent backdrop for showier flowers. *Cerastium tomentosum, Lychnis coronaria,* the many varieties of artemisia, senecio, eryngium and echinops—these are a few to start.

The thick, fleshy leaves of sedum and sempervivum provide another form of protection from drought—the plant always has its own water supply. These plants are not spectacular, but they do have a kind of subtle fascination; besides, they are so easy to grow no weekender should be without them. They share with the silver-leaved plants mentioned above a delightful indifference to soil conditions—a real boon to beach gardeners. Like artemisias et al., they mix well with almost anything else you want to grow, although their subtle, pearly charm can be overawed by flashy annuals. The largest, late-flowering varieties of *Sedum spectabile* will be lost on you if you clear out on Labor Day, but if you stay to enjoy the glorious beach days of September or October, this is a plant for you. The large heads of *S.s.* "Autumn Joy" are a wonderful range of peachy flesh tones aging—very slowly—to roan. As cut flowers they seem to last forever.

Several species of perennials go by the name of sea lavender. *Limonium carolinianum* is a lovely protected native flower of our southern coast, although it ventures farther north. In August, airy sprays of lavender flowers make a mist above brackish waters where it's growing wild. You don't need a brackish marsh to grow this plant, but it's nice to know that you have one plant that will survive a high water table or occasional flood. Don't remove plants from the wild. This and related species are frequently sold under a confusing assortment of names: caspia, perennial statice, marsh rosemary. All are worth a try; the flowers are everlasting.

Consider using some of the perennial ornamental grasses for variety throughout your beach garden. In the mild coastal climates there is a wide range that will survive and most have minimal soil requirements. A few are invasive, so select with care. These grasses can be seen to great advantage in the bare seascape; in a rural setting they tend to disappear against all the field grasses. The fine blue species are especially effective with silver foliage plants and junipers; some of the red-leaved panic grasses make a rich late-summer contrast amid brighter perennial flowers.

Speaking of brighter, annuals don't have to provide all the loud colors of the beach season. The furry leaves of the yarrow species are well suited to beach exposure and few flowers are more brilliant than "Coronation Gold." This big plant may be too overwhelming for the subtle landscape we've been describing; the various forms of *Achillea tomentosa* make low, fuzzy mats more in keeping with our horizontal outline and the early yellow flowers are a lovely shade, less harsh than its giant relative. *A. millefolium* "Cerise Queen" is a taller, rapidly spreading red variety.

Coreopsis and gaillardia can be found in perennial gardens across the country but along the magnificent beaches of the South they take a particularly attractive form. Growing in almost pure sand, the plants are tiny but the flowers are still good-sized and very bright; these two species, occasionally dotted with native annual phlox and beach oenothera, make low, meadowlike lawns in places where weekenders are wise enough not to try to grow grass. Occasional mowing removes seed heads and the flowers start over again.

Perhaps by now you are getting some sense of the kind of landscape you can create, following the contours of your beach property and the limitations of successful plant material. Start on a very small scale—you may not want to spend much time on this if you could be swimming or out on a boat. If you do find yourself getting interested, remember that soil conditions are far more likely to be a problem than salt or wind. Most of the plants mentioned above have the lowest possible soil requirements but most can't live in pure sand. If you want to try some plants with more demanding soil requirements, consider building up topsoil in a raised bed. If you have natural rock, use that for your outline; otherwise, big barn beams can be used effectively. A few defined areas like this make a useful contrast if the rest of the landscape is soft and shifting mounds.

Try to get over your need for a lawn. It is unfortunate that the traditional and uninspired green carpet provides, for some, a particular form of prestige, especially, it seems, when it exists in defiance of environment or sense. It costs time or money or both to keep grass growing on a beach; this should hardly be considered a recommendation. There are beautiful native grasses that can be allowed to grow freely or a wide range of ground covers to provide greater interest for less effort.

If, after creating a marvelously complex dune garden or cliff dripping with *Silene maritima* and sea thrift, you still long for "The Terrace at the Seaside," confine these riotous annuals to the area immediately around the house. Fill big tubs around patio or pool—these gaudy spots of color are more closely related to the world of lawn furniture and striped beach umbrellas and will look best there. This way, you can spend your weekends enjoying two completely different aspects of the plant world, much the way you enjoy the creations of man perched on the edged of the violent, scarcely tamed world of nature and the sea.

THROUGH THE WOODS

When you first bought your charming woodland cottage, probably the last thing on your mind was gardening. What you were concerned with at that point was getting *away;* this little home surrounded by trees seemed the farthest possible retreat. But now that you've settled in comfortably, you're beginning to feel that you'd like to *do something* with some of your wooded acreage and you don't know quite where to start.

All my earlier advice about seeing what your neighbors are growing is not much help here if they're out of the woods and you're not. Eying their lupines and liatris with envy is not going to get you anywhere. Local garden centers are likely to have three solutions for shade: hosta, impatiens and day lilies, and they don't bother to tell you that the day lilies won't bloom without some sun.

Yes, there can be more to woodland gardening than that. You may have to adjust your ideas of what constitutes a garden—think more in terms of creating a whole environment. All of this will make worthwhile reading for over-shaded suburbanites, too; it's not *necessary* to be off in the wilderness to make a woodland garden that feels wild. Here is a great opportunity for subtly escaping suburban sterility without antagonizing your neighbors.

First, see if there are some trees you could do without. It could be an expensive procedure to get rid of them if you don't do it yourself, but your woodland will have a great deal more interest if it has occasional clearings; these broaden the range of possible plant material. Don't make clearings just around the house—it's pleasant to look out across the woods to a place where the light falls; this creates a splendid opportunity for a path, too. Your paths can move naturally around large trees but don't hesitate to remove smaller saplings, vines and brush so the way is open and easy to walk. One of the great pleasures of a wood is walking through it. The importance of the paths is increased here; even more than in most situations they make up the garden, since besides being highways, they are the sites of much of your planting.

What kind of woods do you have? The light, open shade of an old hardwood forest is what we all dream about but it's not necessarily what you've got. It could be a scruffy mixture of scrub oak and pine; in this case shade is not usually as much of a problem as soil, which will be sandy, acid and poor, requiring much organic material. An old coniferous forest provides the blackest shade—many trees will have to be removed just to make it penetrable. In some parts of the country, the underbrush in a wood makes junglelike thickets of shrubs and vines like honeysuckle, catbrier and poison ivy; clearing this by hand is a weekender's nightmare—better get in a professional with a small brush hog or tractor. You may have to spray the vines with a selective herbicide or smother areas in black plastic until you get control.

The easiest shade to work with is a high tree canopy—work toward this by pruning up lower limbs. Besides allowing for more light from several directions, this increases air circulation, an aid in fighting fungus growth.

Woodland soil—except that in excessively sandy areas—is usually good, since decades of leaf mold have been building up. If your forest is mostly coniferous, it may be very acid—even though most woodland plants prefer soil in that direction, this may be too much. It's worth having it tested and trying to bring it closer to neutral.

Even if the texture of the soil is excellent, you may have trouble maintaining fertility for your plants—they will be in competition with the forest for nutrients as well as for water. These will be the main points of upkeep: fertilizer once or twice a year, thorough watering once a week when needed. Otherwise, your woodland is a model of low maintenance, once you get your plants established.

Spend some time wandering through your woods, then lay out paths which follow your natural movement. These can be surfaced with a thick layer of bark chips, which will be natural-looking and barely noticeable. Planting areas can develop from the edges of these paths: Small, delicate plants should be placed where they can be seen up close; big shrub clumps and large ferns can be set at a distance. Here, more than in any other setting, avoid the look of a mixed bed. Learn from the already existing plants how large sweeps of one or two species can carpet an area, then disappear a few feet farther ahead. Occasional clearings with more sunlight will offer a chance for greater diversity, but even here don't veer off into anything too exotic or out of place—we've all seen lovely woodlands suddenly erupt into plantings of hybrid roses or chrysanthemums. There *are* standard border perennials that will grow in partial shade, if other growing conditions are carefully handled, but they will require much more attention than woodlanders and they will be more difficult to place gracefully. If you really want to grow them, keep them close to the house. Your plantings in general should become more and more wild as they move out, until they gently blend into the untouched wilderness.

If you want plants that are both flashy and natural-looking for your open woodland, consider the countless available azalea and rhododendron species— here is where they belong, instead of cluttering the foundations of suburban homes. These are not personal favorites of mine, but even I am tempted when I see them used in soft drifts of harmonizing colors glowing in the shade. Many of the colors, however, are awful, harmonizing neither with each other nor anything else on earth. There is an enormous range available so choose carefully. Many are not hardy in the coldest areas of our country, but some will survive. Consider the lovely native "Pinxter" azalea *(Rhododendron periclymenoides)* or some of the deciduous hybrids. Don't simply dot these shrubs around your woodland—create clusters of two or three colors, with open woods and paths between them.

After the explosive color and opulent flowering of the rhododendron, most other shrubs for shade look like underachievers, but there are many possibilities with which to vary your shrub layer, either for foliage alone or subtle flowers, depending on your climate zone and the look of your woodland. A note on hydrangeas might be in order here—yes, they do quite well in shade, but few things would look more out of place in this natural forest we're trying to achieve.

What is a wood without ferns? They are to the forest floor what grasses are to the fields—numerous, varied, tough: indispensable. You probably already have several species in residence or can move them from other parts of your property. Don't be misled by their feathery, frail appearance—they take moving with nonchalance. Even drought is usually not fatal. You can introduce an occasional note of the exotic by planting some of the lovely Japanese painted ferns here or there.

Spring is the big moment in the shady garden, but you can get an early jump on it by planting hellebores. These Christmas or lenten roses will show up anytime from December until May, depending on your climate and snow cover. The flowers open slowly and last a long time—the peculiar green blossoms of *H. viridis* still linger through July. The leaves are attractive and evergreen.

All the early spring bulbs appear to advantage in this kind of setting—some, like snowdrops, do better under trees than anywhere else. Plant great carpets of narcissus where the late spring shade doesn't get too deep—keep these at a distance from paths and later plantings so their yellowing foliage in the summer doesn't intrude. Tulips are really too formal for this setting, besides being at the top of the most-wanted list of rabbits and deer.

Speaking of your woodland neighbors, this is a definite problem in your setting. Rabbits, woodchucks and deer are even worse than on a rural farm—here you have moved onto their turf, so to speak, and it may be a fight to keep them at bay, since they are everywhere around you. A dog will be some help. Finding plants they don't like is some help—narcissus are usually untouched, ferns don't seem to attract attention. Your rhododendrons make a three-star meal—when they are small, wrap them in burlap in winter; then you have only three other seasons to worry about. There's not much else you can do, except learn to enjoy a front-row seat on nature (one friend can get close enough to his deer in daytime to hit them with rocks—not that it makes any difference).

Develop areas of your woodland in slightly different ways. Keep some sections for only native plant material; in others, introduce plantings of appropriate exotics. Use the shape and movement of your paths as well as the placement of larger shrub plantings to isolate and emphasize your groupings. Few sights could equal that of coming around a corner and facing a great mat of trillium in flower or discovering a vale of *Primula japonica*. Trillium species provide some of the most striking highlights of a shady garden and most, contrary to rumor, are not difficult to grow; they may, however, be difficult to move. In rocky areas, they send down a very long single root into crevices—it's heartbreaking to try to dig this out, have it snap and know you have destroyed the plant. Better to buy them in pots—they will settle in more easily, too.

The myriad primrose species provide a huge selection of possibilities for your woods. They are available in an astonishing range of colors, sizes and shapes and offer bloom from earliest spring through July. In cool, moderate climates they flower almost year round. Some are more difficult than others, and a few definitely qualify as prima-donna plants, but there are more than enough beginner primulas to get you started. The only real problem is figuring out which is which—I can never remember which are *Primula malacoides, P. denticulata,* or *P. auricula.* With more than 400 species to choose from, you may have the same problem. Plant whatever you can find locally and experiment with a range of seeds—most start easily that way.

The majority of woodland plants—the primulas, for example—have fairly shallow root systems; this makes them easy to plant, easy to move. If you find, when you start to dig in an area, that the soil is made impenetrable by tree roots, you can either hack a hole through the roots or build up a layer of soil on top of what is there. Six to eight inches will suffice for most woodland natives. This is obviously a far cry from the preparation necessary for a perennial bed.

Paths are of great importance in a natural woodland garden, since here they not only shape your property and dictate movement, but also provide the sites for much of your planting. Flowering shrub masses are best seen at a distance, but smaller plants should be placed at the edges of your walks, where you can enjoy them up close and keep track of them.

The trees overhead will be constantly mulching your garden and any additional mulch you deem necessary will look natural here—use chopped leaves or bark chips. Autumn leaf fall will provide the best winter protection you could hope for but some evergreen plants like hellebore might benefit from prickly conifer boughs to keep the rabbits and deer away.

Don't feel it is necessary to fill up all the bare spots on the forest floor—these are part of the natural pattern of plant distribution in this environment and they make a restful pause. And don't try to have a lawn—what could be more alien in this setting? You can with some effort make grass grow in the shade, but why on earth would you want to? Let the woods come up to your doorstep—use the immediate surrounding ground of your house to plant particularly choice shrubs and perennials that need more attention.

More and more plant nurseries are offering native woodland plants and others that do well in shade. There are numerous mail-order sources, too, both for the countless rhododendrons and for "companion plants" that share their requirements. One of the best books to help you decide on possible plant material is *The Complete Shade Gardener* by George Schenk. The title is scarcely an exaggeration—it really has everything you need to know to plant your woods. This presents a huge range of shade lovers in such a tempting fashion that the rest of us struggling with our weeds in full sun might just decide to start looking for a dappled little retreat in the woods.

INTO THE WATER

A recent study at North Carolina State University showed that small streams are the number one favorite play environment for young children. You don't need a university study to point this out, of course; I have a not-yet-three-year-old researcher who damply demonstrates this every chance he gets. Throughout my own childhood I spent untold hours perched at the edge of a small swamp, examining jewelweed and tiny freshwater crayfish. This is a fascination one never outgrows.

Pond, swamp, stream, even just a low area that is always damp—these add a whole new dimension to any country property, both as landscape elements in themselves and as sites for some very different kinds of plantings. Any form of water is a magnet—even if it is at some distance from the house, it becomes the target of frequent excursions; paths and plantings can be developed to enhance this route. A natural spring or pool away from the house will have to be planted with care, since this will also be a favorite haunt of wildlife. *Iris versicolor, I. pseudacorus, Lychnis flos-cuculi, Geum rivale,* twisted ladies' tresses—all these occur naturally in damp ground and don't have great interest for browsers.

The essence of a stream is movement. Be sure your plantings don't interrupt this or make it inaccessible. It's important to be able to walk along the stream, watching it—plant a long stretch on one side, then, when opportunity occurs to jump across, move your plants to the opposite bank. At a distance what you see is stretches of flashing water moving among the plants.

Don't struggle too hard with already existing plants. There are a few unpleasant, skin-tearing, saw-edged grasses and polygonums you might want to get rid of, as well as nettles if they're indigenous to your area, but many waterside plants are among our loveliest wild flowers. Thin them selectively, move them, but let them make your framework. They are equipped to handle the vagaries of streamside life—frequent flooding, tearing currents, sudden drying out in fall drought.

Get to know the seasonal patterns of your stream before you plant it. The raging river of April could slow to a trickle in September—daffodils planted in October could be underwater next March. Let fast-growing mud lovers like jewelweed or mimulus spread to cover the edges of your diminished creek late in the season but be careful that the stream bed doesn't fill up with bulky grasses—these might contribute to flooding when the winter rains occur.

If you don't have a natural water feature, consider digging a small pond.

The county extension agent is the expert on this and a consultation costs nothing. In some areas blasting may be necessary and prohibitively expensive; in others, sandy soil may make it impossible unless a concrete or plastic liner is used. Even a very small pool can add a great deal to your garden life, so the investment may well be worth it. (It has infinitely more to offer than a swimming pool, for instance, at a fraction of the cost.) If you have a pond made, consider locating it where you can see it from the house—in every season there is something to look at, even when the plantings are underground.

Planting of your pond or stream poses only a few problems: how to choose among the large number of plants that thrive in this environment, and directing traffic so they don't overrun one another and the pond. I wouldn't have believed that one day I would be hacking away at Japanese iris to get through a path to the water, but here I am. Plants that make delicate, upright accents in mixed borders—some of the Siberian iris or *Lobelia cardinalis*—turn into sturdy giants in this setting. Most are virtually maintenance-free. I have read about the various horticultural demands of the glorious Japanese iris but in this setting I have experienced no temper tantrums from them. I cut all the iris seed pods in late fall; in early spring I remove the big mounds of old foliage and apply fertilizer. That's it.

Marsh marigolds open the flowering season around my pond. Pheasant's eye and poet's narcissus seem to thrive, although they're underwater part of the time. *Leucojum vernale* and *L. aestivum* are two other interesting bulb species, like giant snowdrops. In May, forget-me-nots make a haze of blue over any patch of open ground, until the larger plants get going and force them out. The monumental *Iris pseudacorus* dominates from the end of May until the Siberians start. A few astilbe remain from an early planting experiment but they are too polite for this crowd and should go back to the slower pace of the woodland, where they won't be pushed around. Aruncus, a giant astilbe relative with creamy plumes, is a better choice. July brings the Japanese iris and *Cimicifuga racemosa.* The wild rice then starts and sagittaria dots the water surface with flakes of white. August is a madhouse of lythrum I can't get rid of, boneset and Joe-Pye weed, vervain and startling red spears of *Lobelia cardinalis.*

This is what I can never achieve in a perennial border—continuous bloom and almost no work. There are a few other plants dotted around but just those mentioned should satisfy even a demanding weekender. The soil here is pure clay—great for ponds, terrible for gardens. When I plant new things, I dig a big hole and put in lots of organic material. After that, they're on their own. Some of the plants are natives who just showed up; like the frogs, they arrive from nowhere as soon as a pond is made. Some are natives I moved here. All are thriving to the extent that I can't find the water in August.

If you want a big pond for swimming, it's better to keep the plants out— they will take over much quicker than you thought possible and make it difficult or unpleasant to be in the water. Keep a separate pool for your plantings. A pond for swimming should be deep and have quite steep sides to discourage weedy growth. A pond for planting should be shallow with broad, slowly deep-ening margins to afford maximum planting space.

Most of the plants mentioned above will grow in swamps or at the edges of water; even just a damp spot will do. There is a whole other category of plants for total immersion. The queen of these is the water lily. The huge trop-ical varieties are too startling for a wild natural setting, but would be at home in a more formal reflecting pool. The colors are beyond description and might look a little too much like plastic for some tastes. Besides, they're not hardy in most of this country, so you must replant every year. The more humble but still lovely hardy varieties are somewhat easier to use but they are apt to take off like wildfire once planted. My own experimentation with these was curtailed by muskrats. Flowering rush, pickerel weed and a host of companion plants are offered by mail-order dealers in this specialty.

All the plants mentioned above are herbaceous; for larger-scale plantings, the willow family can provide innumerable tree and shrub species. The red-twig dogwood, *Cornus alba,* provides a vivid winter accent. Clethra is a native water-loving shrub with spikes of pink or creamy white, deliciously fragrant flowers in August. Two vines can be used scrambling over taller material, both with frothy white flowers late in the season: The annual spiny cucumber vine produces papery, inflated pods; traveler's joy, *Clematis virginiana,* has masses of silky, swirled seed heads for late fall interest, persisting into winter.

Your choice of plantings should reflect the setting of your pond. My own little water planting is clearly a part of the garden—in a wild setting or along a natural stream the hybrid, exotic-looking irises would be out of place, but there are lovely native species in every part of the country that could be substituted. This is a perfect way to use them. A quiet woodland pond or an acid bog would require totally different approaches. Gertrude Jekyll's classic, *Wall and Water Gardens,* is an excellent source of ideas for the many kinds of waterworks; some of the plants may be unfamiliar or unavailable but the overall approach has something for every gardener.

One of those three-year-old researchers I mentioned earlier can detail the other delights of water gardening: Salamanders, frogs in chorus, kingfishers, dragonflies, mud—it's a long and wonderful list. Most of us weekend gardeners are still just kids who can't wait to get back in the water.

ON THE ROCKS

"When I found there was six inches of soil covering those rock ledges, I said, 'Drop the delphinium.'" These words were spoken by a great American rock gardener but they are echoed by everyone who comes up against this situation. She was not a rock gardener when she bought her property—she had dreams of English borders just like the rest of us. But when you find that a pick is the only gardening implement you can get into your ground, it's time to regroup your gardening aspirations.

You don't have to have rocks to have a rock garden—some rock gardeners don't even like them. On the other hand, at the height of the rock-gardening craze in Britain, gardeners actually moved tons of rock *into* suburban backyards. This clearly is sheer madness. We are assuming that, like them or not, you've got those rocks, they're all you've got, and somehow you still want to make a garden.

You may, like the gardener above, have long stretches of rock ledge covered with a few inches of soil in which are lodged grasses and weeds of your area. Developing an area like this for planting has a kind of archaeological fascination to it—you want to reveal sections of this natural formation, then plan your plantings around them. At least here you won't have the principal problem of many rock gardeners: getting the rocks to look right. Keep any good soil that can be salvaged from the original covering layers. This can be improved with sand and leaf mold or compost and put back into pockets or crevices you decide to plant.

It's more likely that your rocks are not arranged in such an attractive natural package. What you have instead is just soil filled with small-to-medium-sized rocks interspersed with an occasional boulder. To prepare soil like this for any kind of planting, most of these rocks must come out. You can use them the way all the farmers in your area have used them for the last two centuries— walls, paths, pavings. These can all be planted. A raised bed can be made from your rocks: This is a freestanding wall that encloses soil; both the outside of the walls and the soil within are planted with rock plants.

Any change of level in your garden is a good excuse for a retaining wall, which can then be planted. Small terraces can be built—this brings little plants closer to eye level and isolates specimens that could get lost in a larger planting.

If you really start getting interested, perhaps a scree is for you. A natural scree is the sloping mound of gravel or broken stone which accumulates at the bottom of a rock face. Organic material slowly builds up in the stone mix and plants start to find a home. To build your own scree, dig out an area to a depth of three feet. As you cultivate other parts of the garden, take all the rocks you dig out and throw them into the hole (this is the fun part). Fill the top third or so with a mixture of gravel, sand and leaf mold. (I am going through this in a fairly breezy manner but don't be deceived—it is an incredible amount of work.) The result looks like an unpaved roadbed; you can't believe anything will grow here, but plants love it. Refugees start arriving from other parts of your garden, plants that languished elsewhere suddenly take hold and species that previously were barely hardy now flourish. You'll begin to decide to grow everything this way.

So far, I've deliberately said nothing about the plants—many of the names would be unfamiliar, intimidating and unpronounceable. There are easy and lovely big groups with which to start: arabis, armeria, veronica, pulsatilla, campanula, dianthus, aquilegia, allium, draba, sedum and sempervivum. These are widely available and almost foolproof, given good drainage. Many don't *need* to be grown in a scree or even a raised bed. But one attraction of these plants is their small size—they are best seen as elements in a miniature landscape. Once you begin to grow them that way, they reveal their particular fascination.

No one could say that a rock garden is low maintenance. You will never have to stake these plants and most have few diseases or pests beyond the ubiquitous slug, but careful and constant weeding is essential—it takes little to overrun the tiny plants.

Don't be misled by European books on alpine gardens: Full sun is *not* a prerequisite. Most European alpines, although they occur naturally in treeless areas, need some protection from the sun in our harsher American summer. Many native American rock plants are woodland dwellers. There is a wide range of plants for whatever exposure your garden offers.

In the hot and dry parts of our country, traditional alpines will be a disaster. Turn instead to the fascinating plants of our desert regions, perfectly at home in sand and rock. Consider some of the glorious bulbs of South Africa— flowers have no political affiliations and it's better to know these lovely plants and enjoy them here than in their native place.

Don't be put off when you find that this is not really a garden you can share. Most uninitiated visitors will simply be bewildered by your enthusiasm for a specimen plant four inches high. Neighbors will probably find your passion for rocks hilarious, although some get into the right spirit—acquaintances still show up at our place with a few fine rocks they thought we might like.

Start small—many rock plants can be accommodated in one raised bed (rock gardens are ideal for weekenders who have limited space) and you can have the chance to see if you're interested. If the fascination takes hold, Lincoln Foster's *Rock Gardening: A Guide to Growing Alpines and Other Wildflowers in America* is indispensable. Consider joining the American Rock Garden Society—there are few general sources for the finer rock plants and this organization can help you find them, as well as put you in touch with others with this same obsession. Their yearly seed list is astounding, irresistible for any gardener.

If, after getting hooked on this project, your backyard looks like a highway under construction and your neighbors as well as your spouse think you are certifiable, just wait until next spring. The rock garden rushes into bloom literally months before the big perennials get started—these plants will add a whole new season of bloom to your garden. Tiny bulbs show up here first and are best seen in clumps huddled against a protective boulder. Even a confirmed delphinium grower could be won over by shimmering golden mats of *Draba sibirica* showing off the soft purple of pulsatilla. It's not a garden for everyone; like many fantasies, this one is chiefly a private pleasure, but that, too, is an indisputable part of its charm.

GARDENING ACROSS
AMERICA:
A REGIONAL GUIDE

*I*t's hard to make sweeping generalizations about gardening across America; well, actually, it's easy to make them, but many just don't make sense for one region of this country or another. Are recommended flowers for Texas going to survive in Michigan? Can a planting calendar for Arizona offer any help to readers in Vermont? Gardeners in some parts of this country are probably resigned to thumbing through attractive gardening books and realizing that 80 percent of the information therein has nothing to do with their own situation.

I can't really claim that this book is going to redress these wrongs, but I'm going to give it a try. There is no denying that many statements in the text may reflect the point of view of a gardener in the Northeast or Midwest; the photographs, necessarily, do the same. In this chapter I hope to balance the viewpoint somewhat by making more sweeping generalizations, this time about other parts of the country. These regional chapters can't go into great detail about each individual problem that might confront gardeners in every micro-clime across the continent, but they might bring to your attention some factors of climate, soil or cultural surroundings of your area that you have overlooked in your struggle to grow things and create a garden.

Considering America's widely diverse climates, it's amazing that there are plants—and many of them—that can be grown in all areas. The photographs focus primarily on these plants. Although we weren't able to photograph representative gardens from all parts of the country, the majority of the flowers pictured will grow in a wide range of climates. The appendix of recommended plants for specific uses also confines itself to plants that are widely grown and more or less universally successful. What I hope to do in these regional sections is to suggest some plants that are particularly well suited to specific areas and might be ignored in more general texts.

Two of the major factors influencing the development of gardening in a region are climate and soil, and a great deal has been written about both of these. A third factor is almost as important for our purposes but much more elusive: the style of gardening indigenous to an area, how it developed, and how it can be used by a weekend gardener. In the Northeast, for example, apart from the truly urban areas, settlement took place in small towns or villages surrounded by one-family farms devoted to diverse general farming. These are conditions which create wonderful models for weekend country gardens; several examples of this kind of rural model are presented in the photographs. Attractive as these gardens are, however, they aren't suitable for all parts of this country. You must be prepared to search out your own inspiration—these sections may give you some idea of how to look for it.

Public gardens and plantings are welcome in any setting but they may have little to offer as models for the home ground. Most of these gardens persist in some unreasoning imitation of European models from the turn of the century—masses of bedding annuals (usually unsuited to American climates) and formal arrangements of hybrid tea roses. These gardens are American only in the sense that they are practically uniform from Albany to Alabama, Miami to Minnesota.

They reflect nothing whatever of a region's specific assets or abundant native flora. Don't take these as models of what you can or should be growing, or what your garden should look like.

On the other hand, the state-university systems across America are an unsurpassed source of plant information. Almost every state has at least one—often more—arboretum or botanical garden maintained by these universities. As we discussed in the Plant Selection chapter, these gardens may not help you figure out which plants require little care, but they can teach you a great deal about what plants will survive in your climate and they can give you an opportunity to see plants that you may only have read about. Many of these gardens specialize in native material—an excellent way to get to know your local wild flowers, many of which may be assets in your garden. Make use of these institutions—many of them offer tours, lectures and classes as well. It's all part of getting to know your gardening environment.

After you have been gardening in a region even a short time, you'll begin to recognize the major problems and advantages of that area. This chapter will, I hope, offer a few shortcuts. If nothing else, you can see how very different your area is from the rest of the gardening world. That's the first step to learning to enjoy it.

THE NORTHEAST

Any gardener in New England has reason to think often about the Pilgrims, whether he descended from them or not. What were those poor souls getting into, trying to build an agricultural society on soil of impenetrable rock covered by endless forests of trees larger than any they had ever seen? In spite of intense urbanization in much of the Northeast, present-day gardeners here face problems remarkably unchanged in three hundred years: The soil is still rock; the trees still cover a great percentage of the ground; and the climate is still stern enough to delight any latter-day puritan seeking penance for his sins.

All of the most northern parts of the East do have their redeeming features, of course: scenery ranging from the wildly romantic to the peacefully pastoral; old barns and farmhouses of severe and classic beauty; towns and villages as picturesque as the front of a Christmas card.

There has always been gardening here, in spite of the difficult climate. From the turn of the century until the 1940's, gardens throughout the East were constructed and maintained in quite a grand manner, but it is scarcely surprising that few of these have survived. More resilient are the innumerable country gardens on a more modest scale; these are more useful as models for today's weekenders.

The rock outcroppings and sharp rises and falls of this northern land may have made agriculture almost impossible, but this topography has much to offer the gardener in search of planting sites. The inexhaustible supply of rock has resulted in stretches of freestanding and retaining walls which require only a few well-chosen plants to become a garden. Long-abandoned pastureland needs little urging to become an alpine meadow and the stately forests are already halfway to being woodland wonderlands.

It's not surprising that rock gardening has been very successful here and that woodland gardening with native species has been drawing more followers in recent years. There are also many delightfully casual and unassuming plantings of old-fashioned perennials and shrubs to be seen around old homes throughout the region. Less successful are newer attempts to create English-style borders—this is often what beginning gardeners in this region aspire to and unfortunately it is not easily achieved, even by more experienced enthusiasts working at it all the time. Still, better to aspire to that than the more frequently seen alternative: the low-maintenance suburban lot which transforms the landscape in more urban areas and throughout the eastern regions with a more gracious climate. The softly rolling farmland of New Jersey, Delaware and Pennsylvania and the flat potato fields of Long Island were just too irresistible to developers, and the subsequent inhabitants have done little to change the relentless pattern of front-lawn and foundation planting. It's ironic that this lower part of the Northeast, with one of the most temperate climates for gardening, has in recent years seen so few flowers. It's true that foundation plantings and ornamental trees flourish here, but this just indicates how easy it would be to create something much more wonderful.

In New England and upstate New York, cold is clearly the major consideration in plant selection, but beginners may be surprised that the best winter protection starts with the soil. Drainage is the key factor for winter survival for many plants in this climate of wet falls, wet winters and wetter springs. Water standing around roots or crowns during dormancy will finish a plant much more certainly than severe cold or a late frost. The up-and-down terrain can help a great deal to keep water moving but even that isn't enough if the soil is rock and clay. Underlying rock should be broken up and removed. Heavy soil should be lightened and conditioned with humus and sand. Improved drainage can often improve plant survival by an entire zone number.

In many coastal regions heavy clay is not the problem; here, sandy soil needs much organic material to become productive. Some gardeners in these mild shore regions still have problems with winterkill. A high water table could be at fault in this case; raised beds may provide a solution. There are limestone rock areas in the Northeast where soil can be alkaline, but in general, eastern soils are acid.

The generally high humidity of the Northeast lends itself to the success of numerous insects and fungus diseases; these are more prevalent in milder areas. Careful plant selection is really the best defense, although good air circulation and general plant health will help.

Gardeners in the North become resigned to their short growing season. Consolation is offered by an autumn more spectacular than anything the garden could provide and a spring of poignant loveliness guaranteed to get any gardener out and working again.

Most Americans have no doubts about how very different the South is from the rest of the country; only southerners are equally clear about how very different one part of the South is from another.

Gardening in the upper South—Virginia, West Virginia, Kentucky, Maryland, Tennessee, North Carolina—is in many ways like the Northeast, only better. The growing season is longer, the winters milder; rainfall is abundant and well distributed. The summers are hot and quite humid in some regions but not impossibly so and both coastal and mountain areas suffer less from these conditions. The mountain areas, especially, have an abundant native flora of great beauty and interest that has, in many places, encouraged the creation of imaginative naturalistic rock and woodland gardens. There has long been a strong tradition of gardening in this region; that makes it fairly easy to find existing gardens from which to learn, besides the inspiration of the luxuriant natural scenery. Another great asset of this region is Elizabeth Lawrence, one of America's best garden writers. Her charming books are enough to send us all out into the countryside of North Carolina in search of weekend homes.

The lower South has more significant problems, and the chief among these is soil. In many areas, especially along the coastal plains, the combination of naturally sandy, porous ground with abundant rainfall means that few, if any, nutrients remain in the soil for very long. Whatever naturally occurring organic material there is disintegrates rapidly and either washes away or loses any nutritive value by constant leaching. Organic material must be added to the soil in great quantities and must be replenished often—your plants' rapidly diminishing health and size will show you just *how* often. On the positive side, the climate is a composter's dream, since the mild weather and high humidity guarantee that bacterial activity goes on nonstop; green compost matter breaks down months earlier than it would up north. After you start to grow things, you won't lack raw green material, either; improved soil and the southern climate will quickly produce a garden of almost uncontrollable vigor. Of course, the rampant growth of your plants is well matched by their accompanying weeds, and the fungi that thrive on both are usually the most successful of all three.

The South has some of the most famous and most often visited gardens in North America, and some of the most formal. This prevailing formal style developed in several ways. Early important settlements like Charleston and Savannah were real towns in the European manner; the small size of the plots and the eighteenth-century classicism of the architecture dictated highly stylized plantings to accompany the beautiful houses; this kind of planting still prevails today. The general inclination toward formality is reinforced by the kind of plants that succeed best in this climate and acid soil—broadleaf evergreens of formidable rigidity. Camellias, osmanthus, laurustinus, raphiolepis, ilex, box and, of course, the ubiquitous rhododendron all thrive here and—an important consideration—resist the vast range of fungi and insects which disfigure many trees and shrubs in this climate. Most of these shrubs seem to demand to be clipped into regular pieces of geometry, and this is usually how you see them used. You have to keep reminding yourself that this is not the only way they can grow.

Out in the countryside there is a very different kind of garden but in many ways the overall effect is the same. The land here was developed in vast plantations, usually devoted to one crop. Many of these magnificent estates were created in the image of the eighteenth-century English manor, and the gardens follow the same tradition. It's a great tradition but not too usable for today's weekenders.

Southerners have an understandable fear of the natural world running amok—even notoriously slow-growing trees and shrubs add inches (or feet) a year in this climate, and any plot left untended springs up overnight with a thicket of invaders; kudzu, now a resident alien, can grow eighty to one hundred feet a season. The universal response to this terrifying growth is constant control—the gardens here must be the most highly maintained in the country. This doesn't mean you can't have a weekend garden; it just makes it somewhat more difficult to find a manageable style. On the positive side is the astounding range of plant material for this area—more species of trees and shrubs can be grown here than in any other region of the country. Many northern perennials or biennials behave almost like annuals here; even species which do act as perennials tend to be much shorter-lived. Allow self-sowing to keep new plants coming along.

Spring is long and leisurely in this climate, since the early bulbs may start in January or February, accompanied by early shrubs and trees like *Cornus mas,* corylopsis and Chinese witch hazel. Because this season could provide opportunity for a richly diverse planting, try to avoid giving over all your spring garden to the azaleas. It's true that this large family thrives here, and these shrubs have a long period of flowering, but too many southern gardens (and many farther north as well) suffer from azalea overkill. When they are blasting away, it's hard to see more subtle and more individual plantings.

You may not feel up to serious gardening through the long, hot southern summer—let a few long-blooming shrubs and trees like buddleia, crape myrtle and rose of Sharon carry on, perhaps accompanied by some inexhaustible annuals like cosmos, larkspur, nicotiana or the native annual phlox.

The South has a host of summer-flowering bulbs the rest of us have never heard of: crinum, zephyranthes, hymenocallis, haemanthus, allium, lycoris, nerine, sprekelia. Some species are natives, others come from Mexico, Japan or South Africa. Some are fussy about their original placement but most require virtually no upkeep once planted and appear sporadically and unexpectedly during the summer doldrums.

There are many native flowers from this region which can either be naturalized or used in mixed plantings: asclepias, baptisia, gaillardia, coreopsis, gerardia, salvia, physostegia or rudbeckia. Let plants like these help you to loosen your hand and move away from the formal tradition that may surround you.

Along much of the Gulf Coast, a fair amount of the ground is below sea level. Clearly, drainage is a major consideration here, since water may drain into, but not out of, your property. An extensive arrangement of drainage tiles may be necessary. Raised beds may also help this problem. Consider planting some low-lying areas with the lovely, available, water-loving native plants of this region—the more Louisiana iris, the better.

Mulches can be an important asset in the southern garden. Hard-surface mulches—pine needles, bark chips—which don't disintegrate quickly are useful for slowing the movement of water into the soil; since much of the precipitation here occurs in brief but dramatic downpours, this also saves the soil surface from pounding rain and limits unsightly splashing. These mulches also help in weed control. Pine needles will add some acidity to the already acid soil as they break down; balance with a lime dressing for plants with alkaline preferences.

THE MIDWEST

You don't see many gardening books written for the Midwest. A glance at the climate profiles of these states, with great extremes of heat and cold and generally short growing seasons, would lead one to assume that this is hard country for gardeners; nothing, in fact, could be further from the truth. This area, so often described as America's heartland, is really the heart of American gardening as well. The important contributing factors here are a strong rural gardening tradition and soil unlike that found anywhere else.

Like most of the climates of America, this one, too, must have been a far cry from what European settlers expected; once they recovered from the initial shock, however, they created one of the greatest agricultural areas of the world. Although they brought with them both plants and traditions from the Old World, they were quick to make use of beautiful American species that could cope with summer heat in the 90's and cold of −40°. Although some of the horticultural efforts in these states have produced fairly hilarious re-creations of European models—Holland, Michigan, for instance, where acres of thousands of tulips complete with windmills strive to rival Lisse—much of the gardening here has resulted in authentic varieties of the American cottage garden. Even if many of the old-style small family farms are being devoured by agribusiness, shopping malls or subdivisions, enough still remains of front porches wreathed in clematis or peonies along the walk to inspire weekenders who keep their eyes open.

Northeasterners with their rock and southerners with their sand can't begin to imagine a garden on almost unlimited topsoil. Not all the Midwest has that, of course, but in general the soil is of great wealth. This doesn't mean you can ignore it—good soil practices still should be followed—but it does mean that you are starting with a big plus.

The eastern areas of the midcontinent are still part of the deciduous woodland of the Southeast, although in many areas these woods have long ago been cleared for farming. As we move west into the prairie states, the already fairly level ground becomes even more open and flat. These broad sweeps of flat land have a serene majesty about them when viewed overall, but many view this landscape as simply monotonous. This is one reason why gardens in this region are much more like cottage gardens in the classic English sense—they are usually enclosed, inward-looking, and relate much more to the house or nearby buildings than they do to the landscape surrounding them. These gardens strive to create a feeling of comfort and homeyness in the middle of daunting and lonesome space.

Another incentive for an enclosed space is the harsh, drying wind frequently experienced here in summer. Because these winds come almost invariably from one direction, shrub borders, evergreen screens or decorative fences can offer a great deal of help, besides being essential design elements in breaking up unrelenting expanses of flat land.

Low humidity in general speeds evaporation from the soil and can result in drought, but in this part of the country the problem is diminished by the depth and richness of the soil, which retains moisture and produces excellent growth with less than optimum water. The low summer humidity is an enormous aid in controlling fungus growth—a great problem in humid coastal areas.

Violent thunderstorms (and occasionally hail) can bring diaster to the summer garden here. This is the usual form of rain during the hot months and although gardeners have to be prepared for this, there's not really a whole lot that can be done. Try to limit the number of plants that have to be staked, and stake those securely.

Trees occur naturally along streams and rivers and are found more commonly as elevation increases, but much of this prairie area is without natural higher vegetation. Trees have been planted in towns and around old farmsteads but you may find your garden much in need of shade. Because of the long days of bright, hot sunshine, many perennials can benefit from afternoon shade, even if they generally require full sun. Avoid shallow-rooted tree species and those with weak limbs—these will suffer most in high winds and thunderstorms and can cause more damage than they prevent.

Michigan, Minnesota and Wisconsin, although midwestern by geography, are really more like an extreme version of the northeast conifer region. Here we have some of the harshest cold experienced on our continent and this is clearly the deciding factor in plant selection. The growing season is short and cool, so many classic garden perennials—peonies, iris, delphinium, campanula, lupine— perform superbly here, given sufficient winter protection. Make the most of early spring with hardy bulbs, alpines and native spring wild flowers. Keep winter mulches on later bloomers as long as possible.

An unexpectedly large variety of trees and shrubs will survive here—the Nichols arboretum in Ann Arbor, Michigan, lists a collection of more than 2,000 species. Some borderline species may suffer bark damage from winter sunscald—wrap trunks of young specimens and those recently transplanted. Burlap wrapping will also discourage deer and rodents.

Many spring-flowering deciduous trees and shrubs do well here, but not species which carry large or unprotected buds through the winter. Forsythia and the large-flowered dogwood, *Cornus florida,* are examples of species which can withstand Midwest winters but which aren't really worth planting, since they usually won't bloom. Lilac, hawthorn, and hardy apple and pear varieties have more to offer in spring. Broadleaf evergreens are also not a good choice unless you wish to expend considerable effort for uncertain results. For evergreen accents, stick to variations on the native conifers or the large number of juniper species that do well here.

In many of these midwestern states, particularly the more southern, the transition from very cold weather to very hot is fairly fast—some cool-weather, early-summer plants may not perform well here. On the other hand, the long growing season favors many annuals which succeed in the hottest months. There is also a wide range of prairie wild flowers to be considered. These could be best used outside the more managed part of the garden as a flowering meadow, forming the transition between your landscape and the rest of the prairie world. Echinacea, filipendula, liatris, oenothera, petalostemum, ratibida, silphium and vernonia can provide abundant color and contrast in the dog days of late summer when traditional perennials—and traditional gardeners—have had it.

As we edge westward into the prairie states of Kansas, Nebraska and the Dakotas, precipitation begins to drop. The eastern parts of these states, in general, still delight in deep, rich loam soil; this diminishes as the elevations increase toward the Rockies. These states have the typically extreme midcontinental climate—severe cold, great heat, sudden changes accompanied by violent storms. Although rainfall is not abundant—fifteen to twenty-five inches a year—it falls conveniently with most regularity in the early part of the growing season. Winters tend to be much drier. This means that some of the most common causes of winterkill—root rot or crown rot, caused by standing water in the beds during dormancy—are much less of a problem. Many plants may winter better in this region than their hardiness rating would indicate.

Most of these midcontinent states in the North have a fairly short growing season—even parts of Nebraska can have fewer than 125 days without frost, although the average in this state is closer to 160. This short season is offset to some extent by long summer days and abundant sunshine. Garden activity might reasonably slow in late July and August, but the fall can provide brilliant weather for late flowers and bulbs that can withstand occasional frosts and dryness at this time.

Because of this pattern of fall and winter dryness, fall is not the best time for major new plantings or for redigging beds and dividing perennials. Some plants may have to be divided or moved at this season but this means that special attention must be paid to watering at a time when the rest of the garden can be ignored. A dry period after planting followed by a severe winter is more than most plants can stand. Bulbs, of course, can be planted in autumn without worries of this kind.

THE WEST

You may move out of the plains regions gradually as you cross Texas or more dramatically as you climb into the Rockies in Colorado or Montana. Wherever you make the transition, you will soon be aware that you have entered a very different world of gardening. The continental divide of gardening may not be as obvious as that of our major waterways, but it exists and it soon makes itself felt to those who settle here. The vast area west from the eastern edge of the Rockies contains several diverse climate regions within it, but as different as these climates are from one another they differ much more from the continent to the east. For this reason I'll mention a few major problems common to most of these areas, then discuss them separately.

The most dramatic difference between East and West in America is water. Lack of natural rainfall is at the heart of most of the gardening problems in the West, but supplying that lack artificially often doesn't solve those problems— it just changes them into others. Irrigation has worked miracles in the West: Vast stretches of empty land have been opened to cultivation; what was once the desert has become the glorious Sunbelt, with burgeoning populations settled in lawn-carpeted oases fed with automatic sprinkling systems. The supernumerous happy inhabitants of Los Angeles or Phoenix may feel that it is wonderful progress to be able to fight off the annual summer drought with a wave of a water wand, but there are persistent pessimists who continue darkly to ask,

"For how long?" It's not unreasonable for gardeners in this otherwise perfect climate to prefer green to brown, but it *is* unreasonable to expect that there will always be enough water to go around. Recent severe droughts in both the East and West have alarmed even the most determinedly oblivious. It must be clear to all of us that individual ornamental horticulture is one of the first water-supported luxuries to go when reservoir levels fall. Wouldn't it be better if we considered this problem before we created our gardens?

The weekend gardener must be even more conscious of this problem, especially if he is away from his garden for a week or two at a time. It's possible to create a beautiful garden based primarily on xeric plants (those requiring little water) and more and more sensitive western gardeners are learning how.

There are obvious measures you can take in creating your xeric garden. The first is eliminating a lawn. The second is improving the soil (which brings us to the many complicated questions about western alkaline clay, which we'll face in a moment). The third is taking steps to make the most of whatever rainfall there is: creating wells around trees and shrubs; trenching among smaller plants; building holding tanks for garden use; mulching with various materials. The fourth is, of course, plant selection. Gardeners in mild parts of the West have become accustomed to the idea that they can grow almost anything with watering. Less watering will cut down on that huge selection, but it will still leave a great assortment of plants. More use should be made of the natural flora of these regions. Your garden will become much more a part of the landscape as you use more and more plants that agree with the limitations of your climate.

What about soil? This is another dramatic change from the ground in the eastern or central portions of this country. Much western soil is alkaline, and much of it is clay. Both these conditions make gardening out there confusing to think about and backbreaking to change. Reading about soil alkalinity in the West always makes me grateful for my simpleminded eastern acid clay. Understanding your soil problems may call for a thorough knowledge of polyelectrolytes and sodium ions—turn to any of the excellent Sunset garden books for more help than I can give in this area. Lime-sulphur and gypsum are used to improve soil texture and correct alkalinity. Bean straw, compost, peat moss or leaf mold used with pumice, vermiculite or sand can help correct the extreme heaviness of adobe clay. These very fine western soils are rich in nutrients once you can make them plantable.

The original alkalinity of your soil may be enough of a problem, but then you may find you are making it worse with your water supply. In areas where the water is naturally high in minerals, water softeners are added which put more sodium into the soil—these can make clay even more unmanageable. When salt levels build up—especially in areas of sparse rainfall—they must periodically be washed out of the soil using water that is without its own salts. This is called leaching.

There are other great differences in gardening to be found once you cross the Rockies, but in some ways it is unfortunate that the gardens are not *more* different out here. Too many gardeners cling to aspirations for a garden completely at odds with the western climate and landscape. You *can* make a wild gully in New Mexico look like Long Island, but there are certainly better ways to spend your weekends. Make a garden *with* your landscape, not in spite of it. Besides being a more wonderful garden, it will also be a great deal less work.

Because of sparse rainfall, a different planting calendar should be considered in the West. In northern areas where falls are dry and winters severe, spring is naturally the best time to plant, but in milder regions spring and summer are frequently the driest times of the year. In these areas, late fall and winter are best both for new plantings and for moving and dividing old sections of the garden. Seeds are usually best planted in the cooler, damper months, especially seeds that require low temperatures for germination.

The long, cool fall and early spring practically meet in the milder areas of the West and provide a season for cool-weather annuals and both late and early bulbs. One of the fascinating aspects of the many climates of America is that familiar plants common to all regions bloom on a radically different schedule from one region to another. Calendulas thrive in late August in my cool Catskill summer. In the South they can be planted for bloom in early spring. Northern

California gardeners enjoy them practically year round, but especially in winter. The California poppy, eschscholzia, blooms from February to April on its home turf in the West; easterners look for it in midsummer. This is only one reason why seemingly classic planting combinations often can't be duplicated: stokesia looks splendid with hemerocallis in the South in early June; farther north (where it doesn't do nearly as well) it blooms with liatris in August. It may take time to discover your own garden calendar.

TEXAS

Since Texas contains so many climates within its boundaries, it forms the transition from East to West as well as from humid southern coast to dry desert inland, from rich prairie soil to adobe clay.

The Texas coastline is really an extension of the conditions we met in the East: high humidity, low-lying regions with heavy soil and drainage problems, a mild marine climate. Plants which do well in Louisiana can usually find a home here, and the more southern reaches share the almost tropical flora found in Florida.

The northern panhandle region and much of central Texas resembles a slightly milder version of the plains states, with long growing seasons, hot summers and adequate precipitation for most gardening needs.

The soil near the Louisiana boundary shares the general southern acid inclination; where the deep prairie soil enters the state the ground is more nearly neutral. As we move west, precipitation drops and—a familiar corollary—alkalinity increases. Here we begin to find the infamous adobe clay of the West, one of the most discouraging soils for a gardener to encounter. Yes, it's dreary work preparing this clay to grow anything, but once conquered, it is a soil high in nutrients; it also will yield results with far less water, an all-important consideration as we head west.

Oklahoma and New Mexico share with the western extremes of Texas enormous ranges of temperature, from great heat to terrible cold. Any of the flat, open parts of these states can be subject to very high winds and accompanying dust storms. As in the Midwest, windbreaks can provide both protection and relief from the flat natural topography.

Texas is such an enormous expanse of different climates, it is not surprising that it has large native plant populations all its own. What is surprising is that the Texas Department of Highways has actually developed programs to preserve these populations and, wherever possible, make them better known and more widespread. As a result, flourishing colonies of native plants can be seen on the roadsides of this vast state, an inspiration for meadow gardeners and weekend workers of this region. The Texas blue-bonnet, *Lupinus texensis,* is probably the best known of these beautiful natives; like many members of this genus, it may be hard to grow, especially for non-Texans, but it's well worth a try. Some of the native sages—*Salvia farinacea* or *S. azurea,* for example—are very lovely and very easy. Many penstemons flourish here as in most parts of the West. Argemone, the dramatic prickly poppy, is a striking plant with a long blooming period and few cultural demands.

It is in Texas that we first see some of the Spanish influence in the prevailing garden style—this will become more pronounced as we move westward (there is a small amount of Spanish influence in Florida but it is much more confused there). The Spanish were the settlers best suited for dealing with the deserts of the Southwest, since both the original inhabitants of Spain and their Moorish conquerors were adept at creating gardens in the face of drought and other extremities of climate.

One common temptation arises frequently in all the mild southern areas of our country: the urge to grow tender, tropical material. It's easy to forget, in a state where the median July temperature is 85°, that winters can bring periods of 10° below zero. It won't happen every winter, and it seldom happens along the water, of course; it may just be one year in every ten. You can either take the gambler's attitude that the risk is reasonable, or limit your aspirations a little. With bulbs or perennials, experiment gingerly if you are really set on growing plants from outside your climate zone; with woody material, you clearly have more to lose. Considering the great number of plants you can grow in the southern regions, east or west, without a problem, it really doesn't seem worth the effort.

THE ROCKIES

The western mountain states of Montana, Wyoming, Colorado and Idaho offer a complex series of challenges to the weekend gardener. Although the winter cold here can be severe, long periods of unbroken severe freezing are uncommon except in the highest elevations. On the other hand, these states have the shortest growing seasons on this continent and in many areas frost can be expected in every month. Precipitation ranges from light to sparse to practically nonexistent. Some areas still share the edges of rich prairie soil, but much of this region is made up of spectacular and unyielding varieties of rock. Is this any place to make a garden?

There's no denying that there are problems to gardening here, as there are in most of the western states, but the basic problem is your own expectation of the kind of garden you can create. Forget tender annuals—forget tender anything. The growing season may be short, but because of cool growing conditions, plants known to easterners as spring bloomers—aquilegia, primula, iberis, lupine, linum, arabis—will have an extended period of bloom and will resist an occasional frost. The same is true of cool-weather annuals like larkspur and poppies. Biennial *Dianthus barbatus* (sweet william), matricaria and Chinese delphinium will thrive and usually self-sow. Even in areas where summer temperatures are high, low humidity and cool nights provide good gardening conditions for a variety of plants.

The real glory of these mountain states is the astonishing range of wild flowers to be found nowhere else. Now, no one said they were all easy to grow—adventurous gardeners in the East have been thwarted by some of these lovely plants for years—but you have more of a chance to grow them here than anywhere else and in a climate like this, many more traditional garden plants are going to be equally difficult.

Although there is usually some precipitation during the growing season, most gardening and agriculture is done with irrigation, water for which is provided by the abundant high-mountain snows as they slowly melt. Even if water is available, try to develop your garden with as little additional watering as possible and keep separate areas for native species which require periods of dryness. You may not understand, at first, what these plants require, so preserve as much as possible their original growing conditions.

Some of the soil in these states may be good for cultivation but almost all can benefit from additional organic material. Soil improvement and judicious use of mulches and ground covers may slowly diminish the danger of erosion so prevalent in this region, and all these practices will make available precipitation go farther. In mountain areas a gravel mulch is effective and appropriate.

Winter mulching is indispensable. The pattern of cold periods rapidly changing to days of mild thaw can wreak much more damage than weeks of more sustained freezing or lower temperatures. Winter protection can slow temperature changes in the ground and prevent plant growth too early in the season.

The Denver Botanical Garden has been rising in importance as a center for gardening information throughout the mountain states. The rock-garden and native plant collections should inspire weekenders to experiment with species the rest of us can only envy. Some easy natives to start with are oenothera, poppy, penstemon, astragalus, lupine, aster, eriogonum, phlox, silene, clarkia, arenaria. Bulbs from this region include easy allium, anemone and calochortus.

Dramatic scenery is very likely a part of the setting of your home in this region—it won't take much gardening to enhance this if you let your landscape show you how. It's amusing but also sad to see how the great homes and gardens of the West sixty or seventy years ago resolutely ignored this natural wealth and insisted on creating gardens based on northeastern ideas of grandeur. These gardens celebrated the triumphs of irrigation and applauded the ousting of natural flora by lawns, roses and high-maintenance bedding plants. In a region of some of America's most spectacular landscapes, gardeners have delighted in creating high-altitude versions of the basic suburban plot. Here, nature will provide better garden models than the "gardens" you see around you—a rocky gorge or alpine meadow is infinitely more worthy of imitation than green turf and petunia plot.

THE SOUTHWEST

Arizona, New Mexico, Utah, Nevada and California all have considerable areas of arid, empty land within their boundaries. Higher elevations and river valleys may have some relief from extreme heat or absolute dryness, but a great deal of this southwestern corner of our country can be described by a single sinister word: desert. Economic development and population growth have come to these regions as a result of the wonders of irrigation; it's true, water can make the desert bloom. There are, however, many positive things about a garden of low water use. The desert landscape in America is uniquely dramatic—it's appalling to find (as we did in some mountain regions) that water has enabled gardeners to turn this magnificent country into yet another version of the lawn-carpeted suburbs. A selection of xeric plants and reduced watering will help to ensure a garden of individual character for a great deal less work.

In the best indigenous gardens of this region, the Spanish influence prevails. Tiled patios surrounded by walls and courtyards create extensions of the house out-of-doors and provide protection for more sensitive semitropical material. Here a great deal of green can be enjoyed, highlighted by occasional brilliant plantings of annuals. These areas around the house may require the most care and more frequent periodic waterings. As we move out into the yard, light shade and graceful lines are provided by native trees like mesquite, chilopsis or palo verde; windbreaks are disguised as handsome clumps of Aleppo

The spectacular natural scenery and difficult growing conditions of the Southwest can combine to create gardens of subtle fascination and sculptural beauty, once you begin to appreciate the land around you. The first step is to abandon all East Coast or English gardening clichés, starting with the lawn. Contrasting surface textures and striking—even threatening—shapes guarantee a garden of unrivaled originality.

pine, sycamore, chinaberry and tamarisk. Huge century plants and yucca punctuate areas of gravel wash outlined by silvery santolina and rosemary; sand verbena and lantana carpet loosely defined patches around rocks and cactus set like sculpture.

Clearly this garden doesn't resemble anything we've been describing in this book so far—it shouldn't. This is a climate and setting calling for very specific treatment. I'm assuming that you set your home here because of your fascination for the desert—create a garden that delights in this strange and dramatic world.

Here, as in all dry parts of the West, the soil can be difficult, but eventually adobe clay is productive when it has been worked over with humus and conditioners to correct alkalinity. Caliche is another curse of the West and not so easily dealt with. This is a practically impermeable layer of alkaline hardpan, often quite close to the surface in desert regions. Sometimes there is a permeable layer of soil beneath it, sometimes not. If you have large expanses of caliche on your property, the only alternatives are building up raised beds of good soil above it, which can be done for small beds of relatively shallow-rooted plants, or drilling out planting holes for larger trees or shrubs. In the latter case, consider that the hole you make is really a closed container—it's like planting a tree in a concrete walk. The holes must be large enough to allow reasonable growth. This kind of situation can necessarily limit the extent of both your planting and your gardening enthusiasm. In extreme cases, it might be best to bring in topsoil in quantity and build up a whole new layer of ground.

Drainage problems are usually thought of as being due to an excess of moisture, but they are equally common in desert conditions, although they develop from different causes. Increased quantities of humus in the soil will increase air circulation between soil particles, allow better penetration and distribution of water around plant roots, slow the movement of water through sandy or gravelly dirt. Improved drainage will also help prevent salt buildup and assist leaching when necessary.

Even a garden of xeric plants will require some water. Many of the larger trees and shrubs, once established, will do best with deep watering once (or at most, twice) a month. Most desert species have facilities for some kind of water storage and do best with a pattern of heavy, infrequent watering—this works well with a weekend schedule.

Experiment with dry-climate species from all over the world but try to keep them in groups according to their water demand. Mediterranean species, for example, may do well but may require more winter water than natives. Species from both North and South Africa are worth a try, especially bulbs. Hot-weather annuals from Mexico will be happy here. Remember the extensive deserts of South America and the wealth of plants they might provide.

The real stars of your desert garden should be your own native plants. Argemone, baileya, grindelia, hunnemannia and mentzelia may not be house-hold names for the rest of us, but they are just a few of the beautiful flowering plants to be found in the desert. Saguaro, opuntia and agave rival the reaches of modern art and offer sensational contrasts to less threatening species. These plants aren't going to make your landscape look like either an English cottage or a New Jersey suburb—for that you can only be thankful.

CALIFORNIA

Oh, California—little wonder that settlers struggling out of the southern deserts or over the northern mountains felt they had reached the Garden of Eden when they got to the California coast. Those of us given to climate envy should bear in mind, however, that in a state as vast as this one, it's not just one climate that we're talking about. Many of the central inland valleys and the southeast have near-desert conditions; the high-mountain climate is close to that of the Rockies in its harshness. And of course even the fabled southern coastal region would not be the Eden it appears without the use of irrigation. It's the usual western gardening dilemma—if you *do* water, you can grow an enormous number of plants and create a garden that rivals any in the world. If you don't water, you can still grow several times the number of plants that can be grown by a gardener, say, in Michigan. But you have to think a great deal more about the kind of garden you want to create.

Both the arid and moist regions of California have a fairly consistent pattern of summer-dry and winter-wet seasons. In a climate as mild as California's, this would be a reasonable pattern within which to garden, except for the expectations of a vast number of gardeners. There is no reason to persist in spring planting here, when fall and winter are obviously so much better suited, except for a clinging to some East Coast or English tradition. There's no reason to struggle each year planting prechilled tulips when freesia, babiana or ranunculus can flourish every year and spread. Why bemoan the pathetic performance of mock orange and lilac when an innumerable host of flowering trees and shrubs can be substituted? Because the climate is so agreeable, it's not surprising to find that gardeners can work year round. But remember that you don't *have* to. Let the summer-dry pattern be part of your garden's changing interest—letting a dormant period occur is essential for many native western plants of worth.

The lack of a winter may be a great boon to everyone living in this climate, but keep in mind that many familiar garden flowers need a specific period of cold in their growing cycles. These plants won't be happy growing year round. On the other hand, the huge number of tender perennials the rest of us struggle to grow as annuals show their true nature here—pelargoniums grown as hedges, salvias as shrubs, lantanas as trees, vines or ground cover.

California gardening styles are diverse, to put it mildly. The Spanish influence is apparent, and offers many possibilities; it combines in places with a strong tropical influence to create gardens reminiscent of those in South America. Severe modernism is not a trend compatible with the ideas of this book, generally, but in places it works with the sculptural forms of dramatic native plants to achieve gardens of intriguing interest. Japanese gardens might require too much control for most weekenders, but splendid examples exist, created and managed by emigrants raised in that tradition.

It's not surprising to find in this region where there is so much gardening that there is much gardening of resounding bad taste. Don't let the sheer abundance of material confuse your design. Don't let the natural excesses of tropical material take over. Avoid the landscaping clichés of the overirrigated suburban tracts: beds of hybrid tea roses; geometric foundation shrubs snuggling against every house surface; unrelenting expanses of lawn.

Visitors to California both rejoice and lament about its supposed lack of seasons. There are seasons, of course, although not as strongly marked as in other climes. Let your garden make the most of these changes. There are plants here that will bloom practically year round, but you may find that these become almost invisible after a while. It's the plants that mark special periods that come to have the most interest. Bulbs can do much to emphasize the changes of time from spring to summer, summer to fall. Enjoy how winter annuals, reveling in cool weather, give way to sun lovers, which carry the garden through the arid times of summer. Although a great number of evergreens—both coniferous and broadleaf—thrive here, use deciduous trees and shrubs to emphasize the coming of spring.

Is it presumptuous to suggest plants for California gardens? Perhaps I will just mention that Mediterranean plants flourish here, usually without watering; all the culinary herbs, in particular, do extremely well, something California cuisine has only recently discovered. As in the Southeast, many traditional European or eastern perennials may perform as annuals or biennials. Flowering shrubs and vines play a much more important role than in the Northeast, since there is a huge selection available that offers bloom in all seasons. In a state where there are eighty-two species of native lupines flourishing, fifty-eight indigenous penstemons and seventy-seven mimulus species, I, for one, would make great use of the flora to be found here and nowhere else.

With water and effort year round, a California garden can be all gardens of all climates, too often all at once. A garden of less water and less effort can have a more distinct personality—that of the landscape and the gardener.

The northern edge of California, western Washington and western Oregon make up a highly specific climate zone dramatically different from the areas adjacent to it. The reasons for this are clear in the geography of the region— the mountains run north-south and stop moisture-laden ocean air from reaching the interior of the state. The result along the coast is a climate milder than any other part of the country at that latitude and precipitation in some regions equaled only by the tropics.

This may be the closest America gets to an "English" climate—mild winters, but cold enough for dormancy of most species; cool summers with long days; unexcelled precipitation, in some regions up to 300 inches a year. This is certainly out-Englanding England, as most residents may feel through the uniformly gray, wet months of winter. And of course the landscape could hardly be less British, since most of this region is still covered in dense coniferous forest, giving way to some of the most beautiful mountain scenery in the world.

Although rich in rainfall, this region still participates in the general West Coast trend of dry summer months. But contrary to expectations, and in spite of the complaints of lawn growers, this pattern is actually an asset. A drying-off period in summer means that many difficult western plants and a wide range of half-hardy bulbs can be grown successfully. Built-in watering systems, oddly enough, are standard equipment here; ignore them if you really want to garden. Because of high humidity, low temperatures and overcast skies, even the dry periods won't necessitate much watering for most species.

Generations of fine Japanese gardeners have given many gardens in this region a distinctly Oriental aura and established a high level of maintenance most weekenders can't aspire to. All those painstakingly clipped evergreens are not for us. And speaking of evergreens, why not consider leaving rhododendrons to the several million people already growing them? They do perform superbly here and you can find species and varieties without number, but after a few springs of seeing them around you like wall-to-wall carpet, you may begin to feel enough is enough. I think you'll find you appreciate more deciduous species for seasonal change.

This is certainly a region to delight any gardener. Only the most perverse weekender would bother seeking out plants that won't grow easily here. All the classic English border plants will thrive if enough sun is provided. The soil is predominantly acid clay and often rich in humus, although it may not be deep in places—rock lies not far below the surface here. If you enjoy your wooded privacy, a woodland garden of great diversity can be easily achieved, even in shallow soil.

Drainage is an obvious consideration in a region with this much rainfall and this kind of heavy soil—make sure the water is moving freely through your soil. Weeds, not surprisingly, are just as delighted with this climate as are your plants—grasses will be particularly invasive; mulching can be a big help, and will also aid during the dry period.

Fungus growth and plant diseases can be difficult to control with constant humidity. If you don't want to spray, the best recourse is to use plants with few problems of this sort. With the enormous numbers of plants you have to choose from, it may be just as well to have a few considerations to limit your choice. In the world of insect pests, the slug of the region is in a class all its own. It is justly famous and it won't be long before you make its acquaintance.

Bulb culture is particularly successful in this region—this is where the famous lily strains of Jan de Graaff were originally developed, and many of the best bulb growers in the country are located here. In fact, many outstanding specialty nurseries flourish in this area and are well worth a visit.

As in all regions where the possible plant population is overwhelming, the most common fault in garden design is too much. Try to make your overall structure simple and start with a limited range of plants. It's too easy to end up with a garden like a patchwork quilt. Work out some kind of limitations within your range of interests: certain families of plants you'd like to know more about, or specific color combinations you want to achieve. In general, I don't recommend this kind of specialization when a garden is just getting started, but in this climate where so much grows, the great risk is making a hodgepodge. Once you've established some coherence among your plants, you can go on to adventure with meconopsis or nomocharis or countless other plants about which the rest of us can only dream.

APPENDIX A

Some readers may feel that I haven't been specific enough on the question of plant selection. This is intentional, since I think in most cases you have to figure out for yourself what you can grow and what you *want* to grow. However, if you want me to name names, below are a few suggestions in some of the major categories. I'm listing them without descriptive fanfare. Many of these plants are so well known any garden book can fill you in on the details; some are so little known they may be available only in certain parts of the country.

The dividing line between hardy plants and plants for warm areas is pretty vague. All the hardy plants will grow at least in Zone 5; most will withstand much worse. All the plants for warm areas will survive at least some frost—they may be damaged but not killed outright by cold weather. In some cases, a plant (buddleia, for example) will grow in the North but is much more at home in warm weather and has more of a garden presence in the South; I list it for warm areas. There may seem more species listed for cold areas, but keep in mind that almost all hardy selections can be grown in warm areas, but *not* vice versa.

To avoid repetition I list a plant only once. Sometimes my designation of a species as a clump plant or meadow subject is arbitrary. Many of these plants can be used in all categories—it just depends on how you design your garden. Many, if carefully controlled, can be used in traditional mixed borders. I want to point out the easiest way to use these plants—you can go on to more complicated schemes on your own.

The distinction between naturalizing and meadow planting is also mostly in the mind of the gardener. Naturalized species will spread and survive pretty much on their own but not, in most cases, in an open field environment where they are competing with grasses in full sun. Many of the recommended naturalized species thrive in the garden's interstices—the space between the beds and the orchard, for example, or at the edges of the woods. Many of the species for naturalizing will withstand shade or thrive in it. Meadow plants, by definition, require a flat, open area in full sun.

I haven't included annuals here (well, a few have crept in) because they don't really make up the permanent structure of your garden. They definitely have a place in it, however. Experiment freely to find which will self-sow and return every year in your climate.

In some cases, an entire genus is listed rather than just one species. This usually means that many species of this genus are worth growing and free experimentation is encouraged. Occasionally, it means that great confusion reigns as a result of complicated crossbreeding and it is very difficult to determine just what species is for sale; hemerocallis is a good example. The result is the same, however; experiment with whatever cultivars are available.

These plants are for the most general garden use. I haven't listed special categories like rock plants or herbs. If you develop an interest in those plants, it's time to go on to more specialized texts.

The recommendations are quite personal and not particularly thorough. Don't wonder too much about obvious omissions. Sometimes it's because I don't know a plant; sometimes because I don't like a plant. Or it may simply be that I overlooked it.

All botanical names are according to *Hortus Third.* I have simplified slightly by using lower case for all the specific epithets.

FLOWERING TREES— HARDY

Aesculus hippocastanum	horse chestnut
Amelanchier canadensis	shadblow
Catalpa	Indian bean
Cercis canadensis	redbud
Chionanthus virginicus	fringe tree
Cornus kousa	Chinese dogwood
Crataegus	hawthorn
Elaeagnus	hardy olive
Halesia carolina, H. monticola	silverbells
Magnolia x soulangiana, M. stellata	
Malus	flowering crab apple
Prunus	flowering cherry
Pyrus communis	pear
Robinia pseudoacacia	black locust
Sophora japonica	pagoda tree
Tamarix	

FLOWERING TREES— WARM AREAS

Acacia	
Albizia julibrissin	silktree
Calliandra eriophylla	fairy duster
Cassia	senna
Cercidium floridum	palo verde
Cercis occidentalis	western redbud

Chilopsis linearis	desert willow
Chorisia speciosa	floss silk tree
Citrus	lemon, lime, etc.
Cordia boissieri	Texas olive
Cladrastis lutea	yellowwood
Dalea spinosa	smoke tree
Dombeya wallichi	pinkball
Eucalyptus	
Franklinia alatamaha	
Grevillea robusta	silky oak
Koelreuteria paniculata	varnish tree
Laburnum	golden chain tree
Lagerstroemia indica	crape myrtle
Magnolia	
Melaleuca	bottle brush
Melia azedarach	bead tree
Olneya tesota	desert ironwood
Oxydendrum arboreum	sourwood
Parkinsonia aculeata	Jerusalem thorn
Paulownia	
Stenocarpus sinuatus	firewheel tree
Vitex agnus-castus	chaste tree
Yucca brevifolia	Joshua tree

. . . .

SHRUBS— HARDY

Aesculus parviflora	bottlebrush buckeye
Chaenomeles speciosa	flowering quince
Clethra alnifolia	sweet pepper bush

Cotinus coggygria	smoketree
Daphne mezereum	
Deutzia x lemoinei	
Elaeagnus commutata	silverberry
Forsythia	
Hamamelis virginiana	witch hazel
Hibiscus syriacus	rose of Sharon
Hydrangea paniculata grandiflora	pee-gee hydrangea
Kalmia latifolia	mountain laurel
Kerria japonica	
Kolkwitzia amabilis	beauty bush
Lespedeza	bush clover
Lonicera tatarica	honeysuckle bush
Philadelphus	mock orange
Potentilla fruticosa	shrubby cinquefoil
Prunus glandulosa	flowering almond
Rosa rugosa	
Rosa species	shrub roses
Sambucus canadensis	elderberry
Shepherdia argentea	buffalo berry
Spiraea x vanhouttei	bridal wreath
Syringa vulgaris	lilac
Tamarix ramosissima	
Viburnum carlesii, V. plicatum	
Weigela florida	

Buddleia davidii, B. alternifolia	butterfly bush
Callicarpa purpurea	beauty berry
Calycanthus floridus	sweet shrub
Camellia	
Carpenteria californica	tree anemone
Caryopteris	
Cephalanthus occidentalis	button bush
Ceanothus	
Chamelaucium uncinatum	waxflower
Chrysothamnus nauseosus	rabbit brush
Corylopsis pauciflora	winter hazel
Cytisus	Scotch broom
Enkianthus campanulatus	
Fremontodendron californicum	flannel bush
Fuchsia	
Gardenia jasminoides	
Garrya	silk tassel
Hibiscus rosa-sinensis	
Hydrangea macrophylla	oakleaf hydrangea
Leptospermum scoparium	tea tree
Nandina domestica	
Nerium oleander	oleander
Osmanthus fragrans	tea olive
Photinia	
Punica granatum	flowering pomegranate
Raphiolepis indica	

Stewartia	
Tecoma stans	yellow elder
Tecomaria capensis	cape honeysuckle

. . . .

VINES — HARDY

Aristolochia durior	Dutchman's pipe
Campsis radicans	trumpet vine
Celastrus scandens	bittersweet
Clematis	
Humulus lupulus	hop
Hydrangea anomala petiolaris	climbing hydrangea
Lathyrus latifolius	everlasting pea
Lonicera sempervirens	honeysuckle
Parthenocissus inserta	Virginia creeper
Parthenocissus tricuspidata	Boston ivy
Polygonum aubertii	silverlace vine
Rosa wichuraiana	memorial rose
Wisteria floribunda, W. sinensis	

. . . .

VINES — WARM AREAS

Antigonon leptopus	coral vine
Bauhinia scandens	orchid vine
Bougainvillea	
Clytostoma callistegioides	glory vine

Distictis buccinatoria	red trumpet vine
Ficus pumila	creeping fig
Gelsemium sempervirens	Carolina jasmine
Macfadyena unguis-cati	cat's claw
Passiflora	passion vine
Petrea volubilis	queen's wreath
Plumbago auriculata	
Rosa banksiae	Lady Bank's rose
Thunbergia grandiflora	sky vine
Trachelospermum jasminoides	star jasmine

GROUND COVERS—HARDY

Ajuga reptans	
Alchemilla vulgaris	lady's mantle
Arctostaphylos uva-ursi	bearberry
Asarum canadense	wild ginger
Bergenia cordifolia	
Campanula carpatica	
Cerastium tomentosum	snow-in-summer
Chrysogonum virginianum	
Convallaria majalis	lily of the valley
Coronilla varia	crown vetch
Dianthus deltoides	maiden pink
Draba sibirica	
Epimedium	
Euphorbia cyparissias	cypress spurge
Galium odoratum	sweet woodruff

Geranium sanguineum	
Helianthemum	rock rose
nummularium	
Hosta	
Hypericum calycinum	St. John's wort
Iberis	perennial candytuft
Iris cristata	crested iris
Phlox subulata	creeping phlox
Potentilla aurea	
Prunella vulgaris	
Saponaria ocymoides	soapwort
Sedum	
Thymus serpyllum	creeping thyme
Veronica prostrata	

GROUND COVERS— WARM AREAS

Abronia umbellata	sand verbena
Ceratostigma	leadwort
plumbaginoides	
Convolvulus mauritanicus	ground morning glory
Dimorphotheca,	African daisies
Osteospermum	
Gazania rigens	treasure flower
Lampranthus spectabilis	ice plant
Lantana	
Liriope muscari	lily turf
Ophiopogon japonicus	mondo grass
Pelargonium peltatum	ivy geranium
Polygonum capitatum	

Rosmarinus officinalis "Prostratus"	creeping rosemary
Verbena canadensis, V. rigida	

. . . .

GRASSES— ORNAMENTAL

Agnostis gigantea	redtop
Arrhenatherum elatius "Variegatum"	oat grass
Arundinaria	bamboo
Arundo donax	
Calamagrostis x acutiflora	
Carex morrowii albomarginata	Japanese sedge
Cortaderia selloana	pampas grass
Elymus glaucus	blue wild rye
Erianthus ravennae	woolly beard
Festuca ovina glauca	
Imperata cylindrica "Red Baron"	
Miscanthus sinensis	zebra grass
Molinia caerulea	moor grass
Panicum virgatum	panic grass
Pennisetum alopecuroides	feathertop
Spodiopogon sibiricus	
Stipa gigantea	
Themeda japonica	

*Species hardy at least to Zone 5. Many large ornamental grasses are not very hardy, but tender species will survive best in coastal regions.

Alcea rosea	hollyhock
Aruncus dioicus	goat's beard
Aster novae-angliae	New England aster
Baptisia australis	false indigo
Centaurea macrocephala	
Chrysanthemum x superbum	Shasta daisy
Cimicifuga racemosa	snakeroot
Dicentra spectabilis	bleeding heart
Dictamnus albus	gas plant
Echinops ritro	globe thistle
Filipendula rubra	queen of the prairie
Gypsophila paniculata	baby's breath
Helianthus	perennial sunflower
Iris pseudacorus	yellow water flag
Iris sibirica	
Kniphofia uvaria	red-hot poker
Liatris pycnostachya	gay feather
Macleaya cordata	plume poppy
Monarda didyma	beebalm
Oenothera hookeri	western evening primrose
Paeonia lactiflora	peony
Papaver orientalis	oriental poppy
Phlox paniculata, P. carolina	phlox
Rheum officinale	ornamental rhubarb
Sedum spectabile	
Verbascum longifolium	silver mullein
Yucca filamentosa	

CLUMP PLANTS— WARM AREAS

Acanthus	
Agave	century plant
Echium fastuosum	pride of Madeira
Hibiscus moscheutos	
Lavatera assurgentiflora	tree mallow
Lupinus arboreus	bush lupine
Nolina	beargrass
Puya	
Romneya coulteri	Matilija poppy
Salvia	sage (woody species)
Strelitzia reginae	bird of paradise
Trichostema lanatum	woolly blue curls
Xerophyllum tenax	Indian basketgrass
Yucca whipplei	Our Lord's candle
Zantedeschia	calla lily

BULBS— HARDY

Allium	ornamental onions
Amaryllis belladonna	naked ladies
Anemone blanda	windflower
Anthericum liliago	St. Bernard's lily
Belamcanda chinensis	blackberry lily
Camassia quamash	
Crocus	
Eranthis hyemalis	winter aconite

Eremurus	foxtail lily
Erythronium	dogtooth violet
Fritillaria meleagris	checkered lily
Galanthus	snowdrop
Leucojum vernum	spring snowflake
Lilium species	true lilies
Lycoris squamigera	resurrection lily
Muscari	grape hyacinth
Narcissus	daffodil
Ornithogalum umbellatum	star of Bethlehem
Scilla	
Tritonia	

· ·

BULBS— WARM AREA

Agapanthus africanus	lily of the Nile
Alstroemeria	Peruvian lily
Anemone coronaria	
Babiana stricta	baboon flower
Brodiaea	
Calochortus	mariposa lily
Clivia miniata	kaffir lily
Crinum	
Crocosmia	
Eucharis grandifloria	Amazon lily
Eucomis comosa	pineapple lily
Freesia	
Haemanthus	blood lily
Hippeastrum	amaryllis

Hymenocallis	sea daffodil
Ixia	
Lycoris radiata	spider lily
Nerine sarniensis	Guernsey lily
Polianthes tuberosa	tuberose
Ranunculus	
Sparaxis	wand flower
Sprekelia formosissima	Jacobean lily
Triteleia	
Watsonia	
Zephyranthes	rain lily

. . . .

PLANTS FOR NATURALIZING

*Anemone x hybrida	Japanese anemone
Arabis	rock cress
*Astilbe	
*Aquilegia	
Asclepias tuberosa	butterfly weed
Boltonia asteroides	
Callirhoe involucrata	poppy mallow
Caltha palustris	marsh marigold
Campanula persicifolia	peachleaf bellflower
*Campanula rotundifolia	harebell
Centaurea montana	perennial bachelor button
Centranthus ruber	scarlet lightning
Chrysanthemum parthenium	feverfew
*Claytonia virginica	spring beauty

Consolida ambigua, C. orientalis	larkspur
Corydalis lutea	
Digitalis	foxglove
Epilobium angustifolium	fireweed
Erysimum capitatum	western wallflower
Filipendula vulgaris	
Hemerocallis	day lily
Hesperis matronalis	sweet rocket
Ipomopsis rubra	standing cypress
Lobelia cardinalis	cardinal flower
Linum	flax
Lunaria	money plant
Lysimachia clethroides	gooseneck loosestrife
Lysimachia punctata	circle flower
Lythrum salicaria	loosestrife
Mertensia virginica	Virginia bluebell
Myosotis	forget-me-not
Oenothera fruticosa	
Omphalodes verna	
Phlox divaricata	
Physostegia virginiana	obedient plant
Polemonium caeruleum	Jacob's ladder
Primula	primrose
Salvia sclarea	clary sage
Thalictrum	meadow rue
Tradescantia virginiana	spiderwort
Viola tricolor	Johnny-jump-up

*Will grow in some shade.

Achillea millefolium	yarrow
Anaphalis margaritacea	pearly everlasting
Anthemis tinctoria	
Centaurea	knapweed
Chrysanthemum	ox-eye daisy
leucanthemum	
Chrysopsis	golden aster
Coreopsis lanceolata	
Daucus carota	Queen Anne's lace
Echinacea	coneflower
Erigeron	fleabane
Eschscholzia californica	California poppy
Eupatorium maculatum	Joe-Pye weed
Gaillardia x grandiflora	blanket flower
Helenium autumnale	sneezeweed
Liatris spicata	blazing star
Papaver rhoeas	corn poppy
Petalostemon purpureum	prairie clover
Ratibida pinnata, R.	coneflower
columnifera	
Rudbeckia hirta	black-eyed Susan
Silene armeria	
Silphium	rosinweed
Solidago	goldenrod
Vernonia	ironweed

Aconitum napellus	monkshood
Adonis vernalis	pheasant's eye
Anchusa azurea	
Anemone pulsatilla	Pasque flower
Armeria maritima	sea thrift
Astrantia maxima, A. major	starwort
Campanula	bellflower
Chrysanthemum coccineum	painted daisy
Dianthus barbatus	sweet william
Doronicum cordatum	leopard's bane
Eryngium planum	sea holly
Geranium	crane's bill
Geum	
Helleborus	Christmas rose
Heuchera sanguinea	coral bells
Iberis sempervirens	candytuft
Iris	bearded iris
Limonium latifolium	sea lavender
Lupinus polyphyllus	
Lychnis coronaria, L. chalcedonica	
Papaver nudicaule	Iceland poppy
Penstemon barbatus, P. pinifolius	
Platycodon grandiflorum	balloon flower
Salvia	
Scabiosa caucasica	
Sidalcea	

Stokesia laevis
Trollius
Veronica spicata

BEDS AND BORDERS— WARM AREAS

Angelonia angustifolia
Antirrhinum   snapdragon
Calceolaria
Chrysanthemum morifolium
Crucianella
Eranthemum pulchellum
Gaura lindheimeri
Gerbera jamesonii
Mimulus
Nierembergia   cupflower
Rhexia virginica   meadow beauty

APPENDIX B:
ARRANGING YOUR
GARDENING TIME

Scheduling is the biggest worry of weekend gardeners with little experience: How do you keep from killing yourself two days a week, especially during those spring weekends when everything has to be done at once? In the beginning, of course, you *do* kill yourself; even easy tasks take longer while you are figuring out how to go about them. This is one reason for starting *very* gradually—if you decide to put in a small orchard this year, the water garden may just have to wait. Don't order fifty rosebushes if this is the year you want to work on herbs. Aside from this advice (which no one ever follows), consider some ways of spreading the work around so it doesn't all hit at once. These scheduling suggestions are really only very general indications of what should be done when. The most important factor is your own time and how you want to spend it. Gardening is a much more flexible art than most people imagine. Do what you can, then see what you can get away with.

Because of vastly differing regional calendars, I've left seasonal references purposefully vague in the following entries.

Spring Cleanup—Cutting down dry stalks, old plant material, dead leaves; seeing what's alive, what's getting started: I always let everything go in the fall so I have lots of this in the spring. I don't mind, and it goes quickly. You can start very early in the spring, as soon as you can stand to be outside, but keep sensitive material under a light branch mulch until frost is past. Clear out sections of early bulbs and hardy plants first. This is also a good time to pull out tough perennial weeds—dandelion, chickweed—and grass. The bed pictured on page 120, approximately eight feet by ten feet, was cleared in less than twenty minutes. This is a great job for young helpers, if you've got them: A naturalized planting roughly twenty feet by thirty feet was immaculate after an hour's effort by my ten-year-old assistant. Such areas will probably not receive any other attention for at least another month. Large clump plantings can be quickly cleaned up the same way: A stream-side planting of Siberian and Japanese iris, caltha, lythrum and others, approximately sixty feet long, was clear after forty-five minutes. The iris will receive fertilizer about a month from now; almost no other care will be needed. Don't add the material from spring cleanup to compost—most of it is dry and brittle and could carry disease. If you have a slug problem, or want to prevent one, this is the time to start spreading bait.

Spring Planting: Trees and Shrubs—This can be very time consuming if you do it right—one or two hours for a moderate root ball isn't bad. For this reason, start this project before the rest of your garden. Bare-root stock needs immediate attention; B&B plants shouldn't be left too long, either. Start as soon as the ground can be worked; plant a few specimens each weekend until it becomes too hot and dry. In areas with long, mild, damp falls, planting can continue after the summer, throughout the autumn. Once plants are in, watering regularly is the only upkeep for the first season. Medium-sized trees and shrubs in containers can be planted all summer if plants can be watered regularly. New trees and shrubs should be cut back when planted and carefully pruned their first winter to ensure solid early growth.

Planting New Perennials, Annuals—A propagation bed is the biggest time saver in this area—and a great help with other projects too. Newly arrived bare-root plants can be set out here and allowed to recover while you figure out where to put them. We *all* buy more plants than we know what to do with—in a propagation bed, these can be planted easily, right away, and left until new bed space is available. Seedlings can be set out until large enough for final transplanting. New seeds can be started quickly in rows. This propagation area can be away from the "public" parts of the garden, so aesthetic decisions can be put off until you have more time: Plant in straight rows, mulch under black plastic, don't worry about color combinations.

Dividing Plants—Late-summer and fall-flowering perennials can be divided early in spring. Wait until ground is in good condition and plants have started to grow. The amount of time it takes depends on whether you have space for the new plants—the propagation bed will help. This is a good time to add compost or manure to the part of the bed you're working in.

Fertilizing—Once plant shoots have started to appear, a top dressing of compost can be spread among the plants and lightly worked into the soil. Spread mulch over surface, slightly away from the base of the plants. Don't spread inorganic fertilizer until resulting rapid new growth is safe from frost.

Spring Bulb Planting—In climates with early, hard freezing in autumn, some bulbs like lilies are better planted in spring. Lilies need deep holes and good soil preparation, so this project could take an afternoon if you ordered a lot. Small hardy bulbs like some of the allium can be planted in spring for summer bloom. Tender bulbs like crocosmia, callas or acidanthera can be set out after frost danger.

Seed Planting—Hardy seeds can be started as early as you can work the ground—many will benefit from freezing and thawing. Write out labels the night before planting; sow in rows in seedling bed. This takes just a few minutes.

Later, seeds will need thinning and transplanting. Most perennial seedlings can stay in a propagation bed until fall or the following spring.

Staking—Few spring and early-summer perennials need staking. When beds are filling up with these first flowers of the season, place stakes around taller, later specimens sure to topple. If you limit the number of sprawlers you grow, this takes very little time; you can do a few each weekend as the plants arise.

Spring Lawn Care—Rake up leaves and debris you missed last fall; rake areas of dead and matted grass. When it's growing, start mowing. This will probably have to be done every week. Employ a reliable neighbor.

Winter/Spring Pruning—Spring-flowering trees can be pruned throughout the winter any weekend you can get outdoors. A really thorough reworking of an old tree could take several hours, but you can do a few each weekend all through the months of dormancy. Young trees and trees pruned yearly take much less time. Good pruning promotes blossom and fruit production and will produce a better shaped tree in the long run, but if you don't get to every tree every year, the results are not fatal.

Trim early-flowering shrubs like forsythia, quince, and magnolia during winter months and force branches for bloom indoors. Prune lilacs by cutting armfuls of blossoms.

Later Pruning—Once shrubs have started to leaf out, dead wood will become apparent. Remove this whenever you get a chance. This is the biggest chore with shrub roses, but it's about the only care they need. I generally spread fertilizer once I've finished cleaning them up.

Late-spring and summer-flowering shrubs can take a heavy pruning after they bloom. Removing spent blossoms of rhododendron will promote flowering next year.

Annuals—Late in May, start transplanting hardy annuals from propagation beds into beds where early bulbs are fading. Sow seeds for more tender species for late-summer bloom. Some of these annuals, like cosmos, clarkia or cleome, don't transplant well; sow directly in bulb beds or areas left open.

Pest Control—Spread systemic granules around roots when leaves start to appear. Eliminate cutworms wherever you work. Eye leaves for signs of caterpillars; later for spittle bugs, Japanese beetles, etc. Hand picking while you weed or water is best. Dust with Rotenone when necessary. Use slug bait during rainy periods.

Periodic Summer Cleanup—Cut back spring flowers once summer bloomers are on the way. Leave a few stalks of biennials to encourage self-sowing; clear out the rest when flowers are done. Cut back late-blooming asters and mums in midsummer to keep them at a reasonable size. Cutting lots of flowers is the best way to keep order and encourage later bloom.

Summer Chores—Weeding, weeding, weeding—this is the major project once the garden is up and away. Mulching will help.

Watering—Don't water until you need to. Use a rain gauge to check weekly rainfall when you're not around—one inch a week is plenty for most gardens during the growing season; less is needed toward the end of summer. When you really have to water, water deeply once a week. Use a soaking hose. Avoid watering open areas where weeds can flourish.

Moving Plants—If you have moderate rainfall or someone who can water while you're away, most plants can be moved at any time. I do it throughout the summer whenever I decide I don't like the look of something. If you wait until fall or next spring, you'll forget to do it. The same goes for dividing plants—simply do it when you can.

Midsummer Dormancy—In hot dry areas, this is the time to let the garden rest. Have a few beds of tough, drought-resistant annuals for color and let the rest go. *Don't* water native desert or chaparral species—they need this period of sleep to stay on schedule.

Digging New Beds—This can be very time consuming. I generally do it in late summer when there are few other chores. It's better if you let a bed sit after you dig, at least until the ground settles, but most of us are in too much of a hurry. Cover with plastic mulch after digging until you're ready to plant. Late fall is a good time to start beds that can sit empty until spring.

Late Summer—Activity at this time is determined by your weather and your energy level. The garden generally looks pretty ragged so I begin rearranging things. If you have rainfall, this is a good time to renew beds—dig everything up, divide, add manure or compost, move new plants into or out of an area. This kind of work can go on into very late fall if you have good weather. If all you have in August is a heat wave, sit in the shade and gather your energy for fall.

Seeds—Sow seeds in mid- to late summer for next year's biennials—they need time to establish good growth before winter. Sow seeds for hardy annuals and perennials very late in autumn so winter freezing will help break dormancy.

Staking—This goes on in late summer to prop up leggy late bloomers like New England asters, boltonia, chrysanthemums.

Fall Bulb Planting—Little by little, all through the autumn, plant bulbs for next spring. Small, early-flowering species should go in early; later species can go in as late as you can work the soil.

Fall Cleanup—Cut dead stalks, trim back bulky plants, clear out annuals that have finished, make a last try to get out grass and perennial weeds. Rake up leaves on lawn areas but let them settle for winter protection over perennials.

Fall, Moderate Climates—If your autumn is long and mild, this is a time of great activity. Now you can make up for midsummer doldrums. Areas of sandy soil will benefit from a thorough top dressing of manure at this time. Move perennials, divide plants, start seeds.

Winter in Nonwinter Climates—In parts of the South, Southwest and California, the wet weather of fall and midwinter is often the best time for gardening chores the rest of us do in spring. This is the time to plant trees and shrubs. Start seed both for quick, cool-flowering winter annuals and for next summer's perennials. Set out bulbs of ranunculus, anemones at three-week intervals for early-spring bloom. Remember that bulbs requiring prolonged freezing are a bad bet.

Real Winter—Once the ground is frozen, spread evergreen branches for winter protection. Wrap trunks of susceptible trees and shrubs with burlap or plastic strips to prevent rabbit and mouse injury. Small evergreens can be completely covered with burlap to keep deer away. All this can be done a little at a time depending on your weather. Remember that spring freezing and thawing are the worst problems—don't take mulch off too early.

CLIMATE ZONE MAP

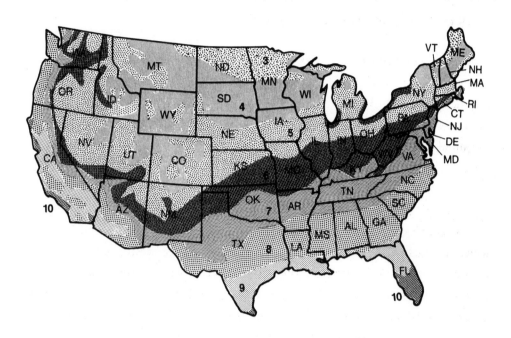

	ZONE 1	Below -50°F.
	ZONE 2	-50° To-40°F.
	ZONE 3	-40° To-30°F.
	ZONE 4	-30° To-20°F.
	ZONE 5	-20° To-10°F.
	ZONE 6	-10° To 0°F.
	ZONE 7	0° To 10°F.
	ZONE 8	10° To 20°F.
	ZONE 9	20° To 30°F.
	ZONE 10	30° To 40°F.

BIBLIOGRAPHY

I've concerned myself chiefly throughout this book with how your garden should look and feel; I realize I've skimmed over some of the more practical concerns of horticulture. Luckily, there are numerous good books to help you with some of the most basic questions. There are also some wonderful writers whose books discuss in greater detail some of the special interests you may develop, and books concerned specifically with gardening in your own part of the country.

Use caution with English garden books: They are very beautiful and we all love reading them, but they can be fatally misleading for Americans, especially on questions of plant selection. Enjoy them, but don't follow them, not until you know a lot more about your own climate and its limitations.

BASIC HELP

The Time-Life Encyclopedia of Gardening
Time-Life Books, 1972
Henry Holt & Co., 1986

Reader's Digest Illustrated Guide to Gardening
Reader's Digest Association, Inc.
Pleasantville, New York, 1972

Taylor's Encyclopedia of Gardening
Norman Taylor
Houghton Mifflin, Boston, 1948, 1986

This has been expanded, beautifully illustrated
and is issued in several pocket-size volumes.

The Encyclopedia of Gardening Techniques
The Royal Horticultural Society

North American Horticulture: A Reference Guide
The American Horticultural Society
Charles Scribner's Sons, New York, 1982

10,000 Garden Questions Answered
Marjorie Dietz, Ed.
Doubleday, New York, 1982

Wyman's Gardening Encyclopedia
Donald Wyman
Macmillan, New York, 1971

RECOGNIZING AND SELECTING PLANT MATERIAL

Trees for American Gardens
Donald Wyman
Macmillan, New York, 1965

Shrubs and Vines for American Gardens
Donald Wyman
Macmillan, New York, 1969

Low Maintenance Perennials
Robert S. Hebb
Quadrangle/The New York Times Book Co., New York, 1975

Flowering Plants in the Landscape
Mildred E. Mathias
University of California Press, Berkeley, California, 1982

The Picture Book of Perennials
Arno and Irene Nehrling
Hearthside Press, New York, 1964

*The Perennial Garden: Color Harmonies
    Through the Seasons*
Jeff and Marilyn Cox
Rodale Press, Emmons, Pennsylvania, 1985

PROPAGATION

Propagation in Pictures
Montague Free
The Literary Guild of America, 1957

Grow Your Own Plants
Jack Kramer
Charles Scribner's Sons, New York, 1973

Plants-a-Plenty
Catherine Osgood Foster
Rodale Press, Emmons, Pennsylvania, 1977

REGIONAL

Landscape Plants for Eastern North America
Harrison Flint
John Wiley & Sons, New York, 1983

The New Western Garden Book
Editors of *Sunset*
Lane Publishing Co., Menlo Park, California

A Southern Garden: A Handbook for the Middle South
Elizabeth Lawrence
University of North Carolina, 1984

Southwest Gardening
Doolittle and Tiedebohl
University of New Mexico Press, Albuquerque, New Mexico, 1967

The Central Texas Gardener
Hazeltine and Filvaroff
Texas A&M University Press, 1980

In Your Own Backyard: A Guide for Great Plains Gardening
Chuck Marson
Baranski Publishing Company, 1983

Gardening in the Upper Midwest
Leon Snyder
University of Minnesota Press, Minneapolis, Minnesota, 1985

Your Garden in the South
Hamilton Mason
Van Nostrand, New York, 1961

Neil Sperry's Complete Guide to Texas Gardening
Taylor Publishing Co., Dallas, Texas, 1982

The South Texas Garden Book
Bob Webster
Corona Publishing, San Antonio, Texas, 1980

The Pacific Gardener
A. R. Willis
Superior Publishing, Seattle, Washington, 1976

Successful Cold-Climate Gardening
Lewis Hill
The Stephen Greene Press, Brattleboro, Vermont, 1981

Growing California Native Plants
Marjorie G. Schmidt
University of California Press, Berkeley, California, 1980

SPECIAL INTERESTS

Herbs for Every Garden
Gertrude Foster
E. P. Dutton, New York, 1969

Herbs
Emelie Tolley and Chris Mead
Clarkson N. Potter, New York, 1985

Gardening with Herbs for Flavor and Fragrance
Helen Morgenthau Fox
Dover, New York, 1970

The Wildflower Meadow Book
Laura C. Martin
Fast and McMillan, Charlotte, North Carolina, 1986

Growing and Propagating Wildflowers
Harry Phillips
University of North Carolina Press, Chapel Hill, North Carolina, 1985

*How to Grow Wildflowers and Wild Shrubs and Trees in
  Your Own Garden*
Hal Bruce
Van Nostrand, New York, 1982

Growing Wildflowers
Maria Sperka
Charles Scribner's Sons, New York, 1984

*Rock Gardening: A Guide to Growing Alpines and Other
  Wildflowers in the American Garden*
H. Lincoln Foster
Timber Press, Portland, Oregon, 1982

Wall and Water Gardens
Gertrude Jekyll
Merrimack Publishing Circle, Salem, New Hampshire, 1982

Water Gardening: Pools, Fountains and Plants
Jack Kramer
Charles Scribner's Sons, New York, 1971

The Fern Grower's Manual
Barbara Joe Hoshizaki
Alfred Knopf, New York, 1975

The Complete Shade Gardener
George Schenk
Houghton Mifflin, Boston, 1984

The Sunset *Book of Cactus and Succulents*
Editors of *Sunset*
Lane Publishing Co., Menlo Park, California, 1978

Desert Gardening
Editors of *Sunset*
Lane Publishing Co., Menlo Park, California, 1973

INDEX

salvia (sage) (*cont.*)
  S. azurea, 232
  S. farinacea, 232
  S. superba, 42
sand verbena (abronia), 237
santolina, 193, 237
saponavia, *148*
Savannah, GA, 222
saxifrage, 93
scabiosa, 42
scilla, 46
scree, 213–14
sea lavender (limenium), 200
seaside garden, 195–202
season of bloom, 67–68
sea thrift (armenia), 201
sedum (and sempervivum), 199–200, 214
  as ground cover, 175
  Sedum album, 42
  S. spectabile, 35, 42, 200
  S.s. "Autumn Joy," 200
seed, 3, 75
  self-sowing, 78, 84–86, 176
  sowing, 84–91, 230, 264–65, 267
seed catalogs, 78, 86–88
seedling bed, 89–90, 166–67, 173–74, 264
  see also nursery bed, propagation
seed pods, 176
self-sowing, *see* seed
senecio, 199
sequence of bloom, *see* succession of bloom
shrubs, and trees, 15, 25–30, 54–62, 67, *116–17,* 178–79, 263
  designing with, 25–30
  propagation of, 83–84
  planting of, 263
  pruning of, 178–79, 265
  screens, 30, 62, 225
  selection of, 54–62
silene, 234
  S. armeria, 151, 168
  S. maritima, 201
silphium, 227
skunk, 100–101
  tomato juice and, 101
slugs and snails, 107–8, 214, 242, 263
  slug bait, *see* metaldehyde
snakes, 103
snow, 188, 189
snowdrops (galanthusnivalis), 46, 69, 205
soil preparation, 16–19, 36, 37–38, 182
  for water conservation, 171

soil upkeep, 181–83
South, 57, 72, 76, 221–24, 230, 268
southernwood, 193
Southwest, 235–37, 268
sparaxis, 71
spiraea (bridal wreath), 34–35, *56,* 82
spittle bug, 104
sport, 86
spraying, 105–7
sprekelia, 223
spring clean-up, 262–63
spring planting, 160–61, 263, 264
spruce, 57, 188
squirrel, 94, 101
staking, 168–71, 179, 226, 265, 267
sternbergia, 69
stokesia, *152,* 231
suburbs, xiii–xiv
succession of bloom, 42–43, 67, 80
  example of, 51, *154–55*
summer savory, 192
sun flowers, 74
sweet william (*Dianthus barbatus*), 42, 100, 233
  "Black Beauty," 42
  self-sowing, 78
sweet woodruff, *128*
sycamore, 237
systemic granules (for insect control), 108, 266
systemic weed killer, *165*

tamarisk, 60, 199, 237
tansy, 193
tarragon, 191
Tennessee, 221
terrace planting, 17, 41, 42, *111*
Texas, 216, 228, 231–33
thalictrum, *117*
thunderstorms, 225–26
thyme, 85, 175, 193
tree guards, 97, 188
trees and shrubs, 15, 25–30, 54–62, 67, *116–17,* 178–79, 263
  designing with, 25–30
  planting of, 263
  propagation, 83–84
  pruning of, 178–79, *265*
  screens, 30, 62, 225
  selection of, 54–62
trellis, 21, 30, 32
  see also arbor

tricyrtis, 13
trillium, 74, *128,* 206
tritonia (montbretia), 71, *155*
tropaeolum, 64
trumpet vine (campsis), 64, *123*
tulips, 42, 70, 103, 205, 224, 239
  species tulips, 194

Utah, 235

variegated foliage plants, *56*
vegetable garden, xi–xii, 7, 97, 100, 161, 163
verbascum, 68, 78, 169
  self-sowing, 78
verbena, *148,* 175
Vermont, 216
vernonia, 227
veronica, 42, 169, 214
  "Crater Lake," 177
vervain, 211
viburnum, 60
vinca, 44
vines, 5, 64–65, *122–23,* 178, 212
violets, 44
Virginia, 221
Virginia creeper (*Parthenocissus*), 64

walls, 30, 41, *111, 115,* 213, 219
Washington State, 241
water garden, 208–12
watering, 101, 171–75, 228–29, 234, 235, 238,
  239, 240, 261
water lily, 102, 211
wax begonias, 76, 77
weeding, 38, 161–68, 214, 266
weeds, 37, 43, 74, 75, 161–68, 222, 242
  definition of, 161
  getting to know, 43, 161–62

West, 228–31
  see also California, Pacific Northwest,
    Rocky Mountains, Texas
West Virginia, 221
wild flowers, 73–76, 227, 233
  see also native plant material
wild rice (zizania), 102, 210
willow (salix), 29, *58,* 102, 211
  cuttings, 84
windbreak, 170, 225, 233, 235
winter protection, 103, 186, 187–89, 226, 268
Wisconsin, 226
wisteria, 21, 64, *122*
witch hazel (hamamelis), 60
  Chinese, 60, 223
woad, 191
woodchuck, 94, 95–96, 98, 100, 104, 205
woodland garden, 202–8, 242
woody plants, 12–13
  dormancy of, 12
  see also trees and shrubs
wormwood, 194
Wyoming, 10, 233

xeric plants, 229, 235, 238
  see also cactus

yarrow (achillea), 5, *132, 152,* 193, 200–201
  A. millefolium "cerise queen," *119*
  A. tomentosa, 118
  "coronation gold," *118*
yew, *57,* 97
  capitata, xi, 32
yucca, 68, 169, 237

zephyranthes, 223
zinnia, 14
zone numbers, *see* climate zones

PATRICIA THORPE has been a weekend gardener for fifteen years. Her garden in East Worcester, New York, has been an ideal testing ground for many of her ideas, and has been featured in magazines including *House & Garden*. Ms. Thorpe frequently lectures and teaches at the Horticultural Society of New York and at arboretums and garden clubs throughout the New York metropolitan area. In 1977 she founded Foxgloves, a custom floral service, which she operated for seven hectic years. During that time Foxgloves created floral decor in sites ranging from Radio City Music Hall to the New York Public Library, from the Lotus Club to a Circle Line ship. Patricia Thorpe is the author of *Everlastings: The Complete Book of Dried Flowers* and a contributor to magazines including *Garden* magazine and *House & Garden*. She lives in New York City and in East Worcester, New York, with her husband, Harold L. Stults, Jr., and her son, Sam.